MW00718488

TRAIL TALK
by Bobby J. Copeland

Published by
Empire Publishing, Inc.
Box 717
Madison, NC 27025-0717

(910) 427-5850 • FAX (910) 427-7372

Other Western movie books published by Empire Publishing, Inc:
   The Roy Rogers Reference-Trivia-Scrapbook Book by David Rothel
   The Gene Autry Reference-Trivia-Scrapbook Book by David Rothel
   More Cowboy Shooting Stars by John A. Rutherford and Richard B.
      Smith, III
   Allan "Rocky" Lane, Republic's Action Ace by Chuck Thornton and
      David Rothel
   Tom Mix Highlights by Andy Woytowich
   An Ambush of Ghosts by David Rothel
   Tim Holt by David Rothel
   Whatever Happened to Randolph Scott? by C. H. Scott
   Randolph Scott / A Film Biography by Jefferson Brim Crow, III
   Saddle Pals by Garv Towell and Wayne E. Keates
   Saddle Gals by Edgar M. Wyatt and Steve Turner
   The Round-Up by Donald R. Key

Empire Publishing, Inc.
Box 717
Madison, NC 27025-0717
(910) 427-5850

Trail Talk © 1996 by Bobby Copeland

Library of Congress Catalog Number 96-84163
ISBN Number 0-944019-21-8

Published and printed in the United States of America

1 2 3 4 5 6 7 8 9 0

COVER ART by Patrick Downey

Dedication

This book is dedicated to my faithful sidekick and beloved wife, Joan, who had never heard of Buck Jones and Wild Bill Elliott until she married me.

Table of Contents

Acknowledgments

I have been accumulating comments made by western movie performers for many years with no thought of ever doing a book. However, now that I have been asked to do a book, I realize that it is virtually impossible to go back and find the credits for all the authors and publications from which the comments were obtained.

Many of the comments were garnered by me from the performers themselves at the nearly forty film festivals I have attended.

Listed below are some of the authors and publications where I surely must have obtained some of my material. If I have overlooked a source, I sincerely apologize.

Authors	Publications
Joe Collura	Classic Images
Mario DeMarco	Cliffhanger
Mike Fitzgerald	Under Western Skies
Jim & Tom Goldrup	Western Clippings
Boyd Magers	Westerns & Serials
Bill McDowell	Wrangler's Roost
Bob Pontes	
Buck Rainey	
David Rothel	
Ed Wyatt	

Appreciation is also expressed to Lance Copeland, Joe Copeland, Don Key, Rhonda Lemons, Boyd Magers, Howard Moore, and Tom Wyatt for their help and support in making this book possible.

Section I

HEROES

One would have to go back to stories of knights in shining armor to find heroes equal to the B-western cowboy. He had the fastest horse, quickest draw, fanciest clothes, sang the sweetest song and possessed a heart of purest gold. Even on his worst day he could beat the daylights out of the meanest bad guy and clean up the most wicked town in the West—without even getting dirty. He set an example in clean-living, manliness and everything a good little boy dreamed to be when he grew up. The cowboy hero provided us hope in a time of depression and war and gave us a moral code to pattern our lives after. He made us feel good about ourselves. While many kids of that day could not name the President of the United States, they did know the name of several western stars—and they could tell you which cowboy rode a horse named Trigger, Champion, Thunder and Topper.

Although the B-western heroes rode into their final sunset over forty years ago, their memory and what they stood for will be forever etched in the hearts and minds of the individuals who grew up in that fascinating era.

BOB ALLEN

Charlie Starrett and I attended Dartmouth at the same time, but he was a little ahead of me. Can you imagine, two Ivy Leaguers becoming movie cowboys?

. . .

One day, purely by accident, I dropped in where Columbia was filming a Tim McCoy western. After watching the filming for a little while, I became interested. I suggested to the producer, Irvin Briskin, that McCoy was too old and that Briskin should put me in some westerns. I appeared in three films with McCoy, then I began my own series of six pictures.

. . .

After I was let go by Columbia, I had a chance to sign with Republic, but my agent asked for too much money. I certainly would have taken less. It probably wouldn't have worked out anyway because they wanted a singing cowboy. They signed a young fellow who could sing and play the guitar. That young fellow was Roy Rogers.

REX ALLEN

Harry "Pop" Sherman called me (before Allen went to Hollywood) and said they were going to rethink the Hopalong Cassidy series. They wanted a younger man and wanted to make the new Hoppy a singing cowboy. He wanted to know if I was interested in the job. I told him I was, but nothing ever happened.

. . .

When I first went out there (Hollywood), I was told, "You're going to meet a lot of people out here that are not truthful, you're going to meet some that are kind of phony and you're going to meet some great guys, but if anybody ever says anything bad about Tex Williams or Tex Ritter, look out for that guy, because there's something wrong with him."

. . .

I was the next idiot in the white hat after Roy Rogers. I was a disaster in my first picture. I wish that I could find the negative and burn it.

. . .

When I started my series, I wanted a horse that was different from the other cowboys. Roy rode a palomino, so that was out. Autry rode a sorrel. Mix rode a black. First thing you know, I was out of colors. So I went looking. I found this stud who was 10 years old. They had thought he would be a good horse for Dale Evans but he was too much horse for Dale. He was chocolate with snow white mane and tail. I had never seen any regular saddle horses that color, so I decided to use him. What I failed to take into account was that shooting those pictures as fast as you did, you couldn't take your lead horse and just run him to death. You had to have doubles so you could double that horse in the long shots and save your main horse for the closeups where you didn't want him to look lathered up, dirty and lousy. I spent six years hunting for a double. I never found one.

• • •

I started with Koko in my second picture and I had him 19 years. He never made a mistake. He was a good horse and I was proud of him. I still think he was the prettiest horse I ever saw.

• • •

There still is nothing more exciting than a man on a horse. Nothing else captures the spirit of this country like that.

• • •

Cactus Mack, along with another one of my cousins, Glenn Strange, had left Willcox together to try their luck in Hollywood. Glenn gained a reputation as a villain in many films before millions of TV viewers knew him as Sam, Miss Kitty's faithful bartender in GUNSMOKE. After I arrived in Hollywood, Cactus Mack became my regular stand-in.

• • •

One of my favorite pictures was RODEO KING AND THE SENORITA. Some folks have written that it was a remake of a Roy Rogers film called MY PAL TRIGGER. But that's not true, it was a remake of an old John Wayne movie called COWBOY AND THE LADY.

• • •

Some of the fellows (cowboy stars) were just lost when the westerns finished for them. There was nothing they could do and they probably never realized it was over. They just got bitter and disappeared. Now me, being a singing cowboy, there was still plenty I could do. And the thing never ended for me. I still live it.

• • •

I'm a thirty-second degree Mason and a Shriner. I guess you could call me a cowboy Mason because my petition was signed by Tex Ritter, Roy Rogers, and Gene Autry. I'm not that active anymore but I'm proud to be a Mason and I'll be one until I die.

• • •

If you're ever lucky enough to be in the picture business— you have friends for life.

• • •

I'm proud to say I was the last of the silver screen cowboys. What an era of film history…it was part of two generations of kids growing up in America. I like to feel it had a positive and moral influence on them.

GENE AUTRY

I was a telegraph operator at the Chelsa, Oklahoma, railroad station. One night this farmer-looking guy, with glasses on the tip of his nose, came into the office and gave me some pages to send. Then he spotted my guitar and asked if I played. I told him that I did and he said he would like to hear me. I played and sang a couple of songs. He said, "Hey, you do all right! You ought to get yourself a job on the radio." The guy's name was Will Rogers. I didn't pay him much attention. I thought he was just trying to make me feel good. But later on, when things got pretty rough on the railroad, I thought if Will Rogers thinks I'm good enough to be on the radio, maybe I should give it a try.

• • •

In 1949, I was recording some Christmas songs. I needed one more song to complete the recording session. I had done a demo of "Rudolph the Red Nose Reindeer," but didn't think much of it. My wife (Ina) heard the song and liked it. She suggested we record it because Rudolph was an underdog and everyone loves an underdog. Well, we decided to throw it in and it became my biggest hit record.

• • •

Pat Buttram was just a natural comedian. He was great on and off the screen. If I was doing a stage show he would be sitting back there, and if I needed a good joke he would give me a good one. His role as my sidekick was a natural character for Pat. He was never at a loss for a good story or a good one-liner. I'm going to miss him a lot.

• • •

It so happens Smiley Burnette is a very frugal man who doesn't believe in allowing anything to waste. One scene in the picture called for Sheila Ryan to pelt him with a whole bag of tomatoes. That evening, when the set workers moved in to clean up the mess, they discovered someone had already scraped up the squashed tomatoes and made off with them. Knowing Smiley and his saving ways, we immediately suspected he was the guilty party. And sure enough, when Sheila went over to his trailer to check, there he was cooking up a fine tomato stew.

• • •

I don't think I ever appreciated money until I had been in service. I learned what it was like to work for almost nothing and I didn't like it.

• • •

On my personal appearance tours I rode a horse named Lindy. He looked a lot like Champion but he was trained for the stage and rodeos. Tom Mix had leased the same horse to ride in his circus. They called the horse Tony, Jr.

• • •

Fortunately for me, I was accepted in Masonry when I was 21. Hence, all of my adult life has been blessed with Masonic contacts. It has been a most rewarding experience—I advise all young men to take the first step in Masonry as soon as they become eligible—I fervently wish more people could understand and appreciate how idealistic and impressive these lessons are! What a wonderful world this would be if everyone practiced the idealism of Freemasonry.

• • •

I was asked by some guy how many movie fights I'd had. And I said just figure the pictures and there was one or two in every picture. I fought more rounds than Jack Dempsey.

• • •

I don't think the country, or the world as a whole, has been in such damn turmoil as it is now—it's a different generation than I was brought up in. They're slouchy. They don't care how they dress or anything else like that. When I was young and growing up, I always wanted a nice haircut and my shoes shined and a good-looking outfit—and now it's just the opposite.

• • •

Give them (youngsters) a trail to follow—something to guide them when problems come along—and you'll never have a maverick on your hands. Even when grazing looks greener away from the path, if your kids are sure the path leads to something—even though they can't see the destination—they'll stick to it. It's all in believing—in having faith. I guess that's the biggest gift any parent can give a child—and it's more valuable than anything money can buy.

• • •

(jokingly) I always hated Bob Steele. He could out fight me and Rogers put together.

• • •

I wasn't a great actor; I wasn't a great rider; I wasn't a great singer; but what good is my opinion when fifty million people thought I did pretty good?

• • •

I loved the great western stars of the silent screen—Harry Carey, Tom Mix, Hoot Gibson, and Buck Jones. Their movies played at the Dark Feather Movie Theater in Achille, Oklahoma, where I put up posters, swept up and occasionally projected film. I knew the Duke very well. He was a very good friend, a talented actor and a fine American who loved his country. I was also acquainted with Tom Mix. He was quite a fellow—a genuine adventurer and very handsome in his late fifties. I rode in my first Hollywood Christmas Parade with Tom! Of course, Roy Rogers is a great talent and an outstanding humanitarian. We often run into each other at different functions and I always enjoy seeing him.

• • •

Smiley Burnette was an outstanding talent and a good friend. He was important part of the success I had. I found him working at a little radio station during one of my early tours and brought him out to Hollywood with me. He could play almost any musical instrument and composed many great songs, including "It's My Lazy Day," "Riding Down the Canyon," and other favorites. We sang many duets together, and he worked in 60 of my movies and accompanied me on most of my personal appearance tours. He and Pat Buttram were the best of friends and sidekicks a cowboy could have. They both had big talents and big hearts.

• • •

I would like to be remembered as a decent, hard-working man who tried his best in all areas of life. I'd like to be remembered as a man who brought people some happiness and who helped them forget their troubles. I would also like to be remembered as the owner whose team, the California Angels, won the World Series!

• • •

(regarding Tex Ritter's death) I was quite shocked. I always liked Tex. He had such bad luck. I used to say that if he was drilling for oil, and there was oil all around, he'd drill the only dry hole in the field. But he was a real nice fellow, and it was too bad.

BOB BAKER

They gave me the (screen) test and out of the seven people they tested I was the only one who could ride a horse at that time. They tested Len Slye who is now Roy Rogers. They tested Stuart Hamblen and four other fellows. They all had beautiful voices. I heard them all. But they were cultured voices—the Nelson Eddy type, like Dick Foran used to sing. They didn't have any western appeal to them at all.

• • •

Johnny (Mack Brown) thought he was better than I was—to my way of thinking he's not. One man's no better than another. Right at the time, he was not as popular as I was and yet they set me behind him. I had my own horse. I rode the studio horse in my first two pictures, but I bought Apache and I rode him for the rest of my pictures. He (Johnny) wouldn't let me ride my paint horse in the series (Brown and Baker) because he was afraid I would upstage him.

• • •

My date of birth was November 8, 1910 (not 1914). The studio set my age back. I was 27 when I started making pictures.

• • •

The only chance I ever had of getting back into pictures was when Ward Bond died and Dick Powell contacted me and wanted to know if I would like to be considered for the wagon boss in WAGON TRAIN. I said I would be glad to be considered but they decided I'd been out of pictures for too long. Nice excuse—and they picked John McIntire. But I didn't accept their excuses. After all, they pick up unknowns and put them into pictures.

• • •

I regret not having been able to physically attend any of the many conventions throughout the U.S. over the years, due to my health. I wish many times I would have been able to meet and talk with each one of you.

SMITH BALLEW

I loved horses and making westerns. I even made a picture with baseball great Lou Gehrig. Lou was originally called out to Hollywood to do a Tarzan picture. But when he got in costume he looked more like one of the apes.

JIM BANNON

I was approached about the role of the Lone Ranger. They asked me what I thought about the role and I told them I thought it was stupid. I didn't get the role!

• • •

Peggy Stewart, without any competition at all, has to be my most favorite gal in the business. A lot of times you'll get an actress who gripes about everything from the minute she steps out of the limousine in the morning till they send her home at night. Old Peg never said "Boo." She knows her lines, does a good acting job, and what is rare, rides a horse like she's part of him.

• • •

They've signed a sensational kid (Don Kay Reynolds) to play Little Beaver in my Red Ryder series. From the time he was five or six, he has been a featured act at rodeos. He's what they call a Roman rider, which means he uses two horses when he performs and does his whole bit standing up, with a foot on each horse. The cowboys tell me he's really something to watch.

• • •

Whip Wilson was not a good athlete and he had an awful time staying on a horse.

• • •

After a couple of seasons Bill Elliott was replaced (in the Red Ryder Series) by and actor named Allan Lane, whose most outstanding feature was a large overdose of self assurance. Unfortunately, he didn't always live up to his own estimate of his capabilities.

• • •

He was the most flamboyant western star that ever came along. If you saw Tom Mix one time you never forgot it. He had a flair for making people remember him. As far as I'm concerned there's no reason I can't do the same.

DON BARRY

I was born and raised in a very poor section of Houston. It's in the ghetto section called the 5th Ward. I went to Jeff Davis High. I made all-state when I was playing high school football. We went to California to play an all Southern California team. I met John Wayne and Mickey Rooney after the game and they suggested if I came back to the coast, I should look them up. They would help me get started if I wanted to get into the movies. That's exactly what happened. The first feature role I did was with John Wayne in WYOMING OUTLAW.

• • •

I'd like to see the return of serials. I'd love to see the serial come back. I'd like to make SON OF RED RYDER and be in it myself and have a Red Ryder Jr. and have a Little Beaver and Little Beaver Jr. I'd really like to do that.

• • •

I'm going to stay in this business until I win an Oscar.

• • •

Audie Murphy was an exceptionally misunderstood person. He was a good friend of mine. Both of us being Texans, we became very good friends. Many people didn't understand him and perhaps that's why he wasn't accepted socially the way most people are in this profession.

• • •

You know, children don't have anyone to copy today. They don't have heroes. They don't have anyone who can contribute to their character building that they want to be like. Today the reason we have so much delinquency is they copy each other and copy what they see on the screen. They think they're cute and different when they're acting like a bunch of sheep.

REX BELL

If you are thinking of entering upon a screen career—you should have sufficient money in the bank to support you for at least one year and a return ticket in your purse. If you finally get a break and land a fair part—do your best in every little bit given you. If that doesn't get you anywhere, then take that return ticket and go home.

SAMMY BAUGH

Duncan Renaldo is one I'll never forget, he helped me more than anybody. He was just great. I was studying lines of dialogue I didn't need and Duncan told me not to read all that as they will tell me what to say when the time comes for each of my scenes. So, I didn't waste any more nights. Also, he would give me tips and advice: how to come through a door and push my hat back, what to do with my hands, where to stop, how to turn and other bits of business. He really directed me.

(author's note: Baugh made only a serial, KING OF THE TEXAS RANGERS.)

BILL "COWBOY RAMBLER" BOYD

Art Davis and I went over to see Tex (Ritter). Tex had just come in from Universal Pictures where he'd been fired. Tex said, "I guess I'll have to go see Sig Neufeld at PRC." The next thing he had a deal making pictures with Dave O'Brien.

WILLIAM (HOPPY) BOYD

I avoid that stupid type of cowhand—I try to speak intelligently. The moment I started acting I'm out of character. Hoppy is part philosopher, part doctor, part minister—he's everything.

· · ·

Until 1935 I was a dual personality. I had a good side and a bad side. I fought the bad side but I couldn't win. Then I became Hopalong and the good side won—I lost the identity of Bill Boyd, and I'm grateful I did.

· · ·

When you've got kids looking up to you, when you've got parents saying what a wonderful guy Hoppy is, what do you do? You have to be a wonderful guy.

· · ·

The kids love Hopalong, and to tell you the truth, I, myself, consider him a great guy.

· · ·

It's a great life if you don't weaken, this motion picture

business. I'm certainly glad I had a try at it.

• • •

(When approached by David O. Selznick about a role in DUEL IN THE SUN, and when told he would play the role of a character who gets shot in a saloon). No thanks, the kids wouldn't like it. I'd rather be a hero to them.

JOHNNY MACK BROWN

Most of my Hackel pictures weren't that good. They were cheap pictures just thrown together. I don't know where he got his leading ladies. The first time anyone ever saw them was when I was supposed to do a scene with one of them. After the picture was over you never saw them again. I had been used to working with actresses like Mary Pickford, Joan Crawford and Mae West.

• • •

I'll never forget a scene I did with Mae West: It was a love scene. I had to shower Mae with kisses. I told her afterwards, "Miss West, kissing you is intoxicating." She (jokingly) shoved me away and said, "Well, I don't want to turn you into a drunk in only one night."

• • •

The films we made had a good plot and a lot of action. We had people tumbling over cliffs and swimming rivers. TV does the whole thing in a room and they film it in two days. They just let the characters *talk*. You've got New York actors in western hats who don't know what a cow is—standing around talking.

• • •

(regarding his small and demeaning role in the 1965 film, APACHE UPRISING, for producer A. C. Lyles) I'm grateful to him because I know damn well that he doesn't need me, and I can sure use the money, but how big can a role be for a fat old man like me?

• • •

Don't feel sorry for me after I'm gone. I've had a full life and I've done just about everything a man could want to do.

ROD CAMERON

I made 400 episodes of three different TV detective series, but every time I went for a movie part the casting directors would always say, "Oh yes, you're Rod Cameron, the cowboy."

• • •

I don't know who started the rumor that I doubled for Buck Jones; I never even met the man.

• • •

We used to do 25 pages of dialogue and three or four fist fights a day when we made those films (B-westerns). We'd make a whole movie in eight days. Today, some of the actors say, "Oh, two pages of dialogue, I can't possibly do that in one day."

SUNSET CARSON

Smiley (Burnette) was kinda cold for our first couple of films and, as a newcomer, you could get pretty nervous working with a guy who'd been in these westerns a long time. I don't know if he was told to or not, but he kinda softened up around the last picture.

• • •

I would have loved to have had Gabby Hayes in my pictures. He was not only funny, he was an actor who could make you cry. Gabby was the measuring stick with which to judge all the other sidekicks. He was always a gentleman...and he was a pretty sharp dresser.

• • •

Smiley Burnette didn't own his horse, Ringeye, the one he rode all the time in the movies. It belonged to the studio and the ring around its eye was just painted on with one of those little brushes that came in those little bottles of shoe polish. Smiley rode all over the horse, but he stayed on.

• • •

Cactus really liked to run. In the picture BELLS OF ROSARITA, where I'm riding with the other cowboys—if you notice, you'll see that I'm having to hold Cactus back.

• • •

One day I was out on the set with Roy Barcroft and Monte Hale. We were having lunch when Monte pulled out his pistol and said, "Don't move Roy; there's a snake crawling out from the rock where you are sitting." Old Roy said, "Don't shoot it Monte; it may be someone from the front office."

• • •

Charlie King and I were on tour in this little town in

Oklahoma. One morning after breakfast we were headed back to the car when two kids came walking down the road. They looked us over and one said, "Yeah, that's Sunset Carson!" The other one said, "And that's that mean old badman; let's get him!" They picked up some rocks and started throwing them at old Charlie. He had to run to the car for cover.

• • •

My pictures for Republic were pretty good, but the ones after that weren't worth a dime.

• • •

My real name was Mickey Harrison, but Republic thought the name was too long for the marquee. They came up with Carson for my last name. Then, they kicked around several combinations like "Cody" Carson and others. Well, old man Yates looked out the window and saw a used car lot with a sign that read "Sunset Motors." he named me after that used car lot. I'm glad he didn't name me "Motors" Carson.

GARY COOPER

I recognized my limitations. For instance, I never tried Shakespeare.That's because I look funny in tights.

• • •

"Yup" is a convenient word, and I've learned people don't expect too much from a man with a one-word vocabulary. Now that I think of it, it's come in handy when people ask me personal questions, they don't expect an answer.

RAY CORRIGAN

Leonard Slye, or Roy Rogers as we know him, always said to me, "Ray, if I ever get a horse I want to call him Trigger." At that time, I had thirty-one horses. Among those were three beautiful palominos—I'd had Roy practice different mounts while at my ranch. The next day I brought Roy and a couple of my palominos to the lot. I gave one of the palominos the sign and he started running at full speed towards the other horses. Just as the horse got to where Sol Siegel (Producer) and I were standing, Roy made a beautiful mount into the saddle—well, they liked him very much and put him under contract—that's the beginning of

Roy Rogers. I sold Roy the two palominos for $500—that's for both—$250 a piece. A millionaire from Texas offered $50,000 for the one with four white stockings, the horse you know as Trigger—Roy named both of the horses Trigger—and folks, until this day he still owes me $250.

(author's note: Roy Rogers completely disputes Corrigan's story; see Rogers' comments in this book.)

• • •

During the time I was one of the Three Mesquiteers and needing a change of pace, I went on a hunting trip and stumbled on this picturesque and peaceful spot in the Simi Valley. In 1937, I bought the ranch, all 2,000 acres of it. That is now Corriganville Movie Ranch.

BUSTER CRABBE

I thought Fuzzy St. John was the funniest of all western sidekicks, and that includes Gabby Hayes and Smiley Burnette.

• • •

Fuzzy could ride a horse; he could ride a bicycle; he could ride anything—especially a bicycle. Fuzzy had remarkable coordination. He was a little guy and early in his career he would put on a dress and double the ladies.

• • •

Some say my acting rose to the level of incompetence and then leveled off. I was a lot better actor than people gave me credit for. I didn't have any training, but I feel if I had been given the chance I could have become a really good, top-rate actor. I didn't make it like a Gable or Boyer. But I wonder what would have happened if things had been different.

• • •

If you can believe it, we started my last movie for PRC on Monday and had it in the can on Thursday! That's when I decided I'd had enough and quit. I went in and told them I was through. They didn't even bat an eye. The next thing I knew they had replaced me with Lash LaRue.

KEN CURTIS

I took Frank Sinatra's place when he left Tommy Dorsey's

band. My real name is Curtis Gates, but Tommy didn't like the name and changed it to Ken Curtis. I thought it was kind of funny because I had a brother named Ken.

• • •

I made some singing westerns with Big Boy Williams. He was a big old lovable lug and a lot of fun to be around. He was an easy going guy, but, you didn't want to cross him.

BOB CUSTER

I was never with the Miller Brothers 101 Ranch but did visit it. A friend of mine who did many pictures with me was in it for years. I refer to Bud Osborne. On their roster was Smoke Padgett, a black man. Smoke would bet he could bite the fetlock of a wild mustang's hind legs. He was quite a cowboy.

ART DAVIS

I went to Hollywood to work for Gene Autry. After a while I returned with my band to Oklahoma. Gene wrote me a letter and said, "I had dinner with Herbert Yates and Sol Seigel the other day and they were talking about making a new series. I mentioned your name." Gene wrote back later and said Republic finally decided on a fellow named Don Barry.

• • •

(regarding his five marriages) All my wives were excellent housekeepers. Every time I got divorced, my wife kept the house.

• • •

I played fiddle for quite a while for Gene Autry. He was a great boss and taught me a lot. It was Gene who got me in pictures. I learned so much from Gene. I'd have to help him tune his guitar—but I sure didn't have to help him count his money.

EDDIE DEAN

I did nine Hopalong Cassidy pictures. I sang in some of them, which Hoppy didn't like. I told Hoppy one day I knew how he felt about singing in his pictures and I didn't want to sing in them any more.

* * *

When I started my series, Emmett Lynn was my sidekick. Almost immediately there was a conflict between Bob Tansey, the producer and director, and Emmett walked off the set. I told him, "Emmett you're not walking out on the studio—you're walking out on me." He said, "Eddie, I'll stay for you until you can find somebody else." Emmett and I did three pictures together and then we hired Roscoe Ates. Roscoe (Soapy) Ates could ride a horse just fine. He had an old horse the studio picked out for him. He Just loved that old horse. I think he used the same horse in all our pictures.

* * *

Glenn Strange was a special friend of mine. Glenn had been one of the top men with the musical group, The Arizona Rangers. He was a fiddle player and a singer. He and I wrote "On the Banks of the Sunny San Juan."

* * *

I was approached about running for the Governor of Texas. I had good name recognition at the time and another singer had been elected Governor of Louisiana—that was Jimmie Davis. I met with the committee and told them if I ran I would be my own man and not a puppet politician. They still wanted me to run. I believe I would have had a good chance of winning, but I decided not to run. That may have been the biggest mistake of my life.

* * *

Making the westerns was the highlight of my career. I never met a single performer I didn't like.

BILL ELLIOTT

I guess I helped invent the adult westerns. But, luckily, the kids never noticed.

* * *

I do not. (Elliott's response to a divorce court judge when asked if Elliott believed in the seventh commandment—adultery).

* * *

I got all the westerns Duke Wayne didn't want.

* * *

I've always had a particularly soft spot for MOONLIGHT ON THE PRAIRIE (a Dick Foran film), because it gave me

my first real break in horse operas. No, I wasn't the hero—
in fact I got myself killed halfway through—but I did play the
hero's pal and had a chance to get in some good western
action before they polished me off.

JAMES ELLISON

Bill Boyd had been a star before he became Hopalong
Cassidy. He expected to be treated like a star and he
deserved to be treated like a star. He was always nice and
helpful to me. He was not a good rider and he never
claimed to be.

• • •

I found myself thinking about the construction business
even when I was supposed to be acting. I had no illusions
about my abilities on the screen. I think I will be remembered more for Ellison Drive, which I developed in Beverly
Hills, than I will for my pictures.

DICK FORAN

The horse I feared most was a palomino stallion they had
me ride when I was back in Philadelphia a few years ago.
A live television series had been planned with the hero
being cast as a cross between Superman and Tex Ritter—
Anyhow, this horse belonged to a girl who could go right up
to him and ride him away as gentle as a golf cart, but every
time I'd even get near him he'd go nuts and start rearing
and pawing the air. Never did make friends with that one
and when they decided not to go ahead with the series I
figured it was just as well. I called him (the horse) something very uncomplimentary!

• • •

I think FORT APACHE was the best western ever made.
Most of the people on the set were calling John Ford,
"Captain", but I knew him from way back so I went up to him
and said, "Jack, are you sure you want all that clattering
and banging going on in the background during my song?"
He told me, "You sing; I'll direct the picture!" Well, when we
heard the song on the soundtrack those background
noises came across just like the authentic sounds you'd
hear around a calvary fort. I guess Ford really knew what
he was doing.

HOOT GIBSON

Tom Mix and I kept getting married, and the California divorce laws kept halving our holdings every time we got divorced. I lost four million dollars. I think Tom lost more.

• • •

(regarding his job as a pitchman for chinchilla sales) All these people would come out to see me and would get sold chinchillas. I was getting three hundred dollars a week and expenses to travel around the country. To come up with more chinchillas, the Astro-Blue people started crossing them with rats and rabbits. The strain became so impure you would have long ears or a ratlike tail. I got out of it as soon as I learned what they were doing.

• • •

(Gibson started in films as an extra. One day he was asked if he'd let a horse drag him for five dollars, Gibson replied) Make it ten dollars, and I'll let him kick me to death.

• • •

I know of no other business where merit is rewarded like it is in the movies—but merit must be aided by labor, and plenty of it.

KIRBY GRANT

Let me tell you Smiley Burnette was one of the greediest guys I've ever known. He'd buy bolts of that black-check-ered cloth - like those shirts he wore in his movies. He would cut little strips and tape them on a card with his autograph and sell them for a quarter each. Back then a quarter was worth something. He would also stay at acquaintance's homes when he toured the country—anything to save a buck—that was Smiley.

• • •

I never wanted to be a cowboy star. I hated it and did everything I could to get out of it. I was a musician and wanted to do musicals and comedies, but they stuck me in those lousy, stinking oaters.

• • •

I enjoyed very much working with Fuzzy Knight. Unlike some of the other sidekicks who were not so funny, Fuzzy was really funny. Much of what he did was improvised right on the set. Fuzzy was pretty much the same on and off the set. Unlike myself, I think Fuzzy was pretty well pleased to be in the westerns.

MONTE HALE

They wrote a picture for me called DON'T FENCE ME IN. It was to have Roy's cast in it: Gabby Hayes, Dale Evans, The Sons of the Pioneers—the whole bunch. This was when they thought Roy was going into the Army. I studied that script day and night, and learned every part in it. Then one day they called me up to the office and told me Roy was not going into service and I was not going to make the movie. Roy wanted to make it. I don't mind telling you—it broke my heart.

• • •

They had me sing a little song or two here and there. But, it was no big thing. I would have preferred not to have sung in a western. I'd rather have done a straight western instead of picking up a damned old guitar from behind the bushes and sing a song before I went after somebody. I mean just all action without the songs would have been better.

• • •

I didn't work at my craft the way I should have, but at the time I really didn't give a damn about it. I couldn't wait to get one of those silly stupid things out of the way so I could go on the road and make some money and meet real people.

• • •

I had no business in the movies. I should have stayed right down in Texas on the ranch. I always said I was born to plow. I was just lucky that I got the chance to make pictures. I feel like I was blessed by the Lord.

• • •

Eddie Dean and Rex Allen are the two greatest singers I've heard in their field. I could never hold a light to them; they're fantastic.

• • •

I take off my hat to Yakima Canutt because he is one of those unsung guys who have a heap to do with the success of western movies, but stay in the background while some of the rest of us get the billing and take the bows—Yak's done more for westerns than any one man I can name.

• • •

I always got along with Rocky Lane. You just couldn't take him too seriously.

• • •

I was on a train with Roscoe Fawcett, publisher of Fawcett comic books. We made a deal for my comic books right there on the train. Those royalty checks came in mighty handy.

• • •

I went over to the studio with Chill Wills who was auditioning for the movie GIANT. The next day I got a call from George Stevens who offered me a part in the movie because he liked the way I put on my hat.

• • •

I'd like to recite a little thing I wrote. I guess you could say it's my philosophy of life: "Life is like a journey, taken on a train, with a pair of travelers, at each window pane. I may sit beside you, the whole journey through, or I may sit elsewhere, never knowing you, but if fate should mark us, to sit there side by side, let's be pleasant travelers, because it's such a short old ride."

JOHN HART

Clayton Moore had the Lone Ranger role and Clayton wanted a big raise. The studio wouldn't give it to him, so they had to find someone else. I was tall, athletic, and a pretty good rider; and I guess I looked good enough in the suit, so they gave me the part. It was just another job to me, but Clayton thinks he is the Lone Ranger.

• • •

Silver was the most beautiful white horse you ever saw. He was very spirited and it took us a little while to become acquainted, but after that we got along fine. He was a magnificent animal.

WILLIAM S. HART

I always loved the old West. That's why I tried to dress, look and act like a real cowboy.

• • •

I am pretty sentimental. The chief reason for my success was my mother. She was—well, just mother. I went to her with all my troubles and came to her for advice all my life. If you have a good mother, I would advise you to do the same.

RUSSELL HAYDEN

Harry "Pop" Sherman had read the Hopalong Cassidy books. When he was in New York, he met Mulford (author of the Cassidy books). They signed a contract on a piece of toilet paper, and they both lived up to it. Harry kept the piece of toilet paper. I saw it!

• • •

Bill Boyd hated the singing cowboys because he couldn't sing. He thought it was a gimmick. He used to say, "Look at those idiots; they got their monkey suits on." And he was the biggest monkey in the world actually, when you start to analyze it. Look what he wore: a black hat, a black outfit with white hair and a white horse, a silver saddle. Now, how corny can you get?

• • •

Bill Boyd was a tough guy to work with. Finally, George Hayes said he couldn't stand anymore, so he went to work at Republic with Roy Rogers.

TIM HOLT

Sure, a cowboy's closest friend was his gun. But he didn't use it to shoot people. He used it against rattlesnakes and coyotes, and for food for the table. All that shooting in the cowboy pictures is exaggerated. But when we used it, we'd never show a man fall in the street if he was shot. We showed killing to be a terrible thing, not something exciting. Unlike today, blood and gore and sadism were carefully avoided.

• • •

They always used to leave the stunts and the fights until the last day of the picture so if you did get hurt you wouldn't hold up production.

• • •

The type of picture we made was family entertainment, and when television first started it then became the family entertainment. Our market left us. It just wasn't economically feasible to make the pictures.

• • •

Actually, I never did like Hollywood. I never did feel there was anything mystical about it. My favorite role was THE MAGNIFICENT AMBERSONS. I liked it because it was a serious part and different from the western roles I usually played.

. . .

In the old days, when you had Gene Autry and Roy Rogers and Hoppy, you would see kids on the front lawn playing. They identified themselves with those characters. Nowadays, kids don't have anybody to identify with. Clint Eastwood and Lee Marvin are two real friends of mine, but I sure wouldn't want my kids identifying with them.

. . .

Yesterday's films were a lesson in morality. Today's films are a lesson in immorality. Today the hero is a dishonest carouser, who would rather shoot an opponent in the back than arrest him.

. . .

They talk about realism. In today's movies, they'll beat a man up, kick him down a flight of stairs, break a board over his head and then shoot him, and he'll still be fighting. Now is that realism? Just how much punishment do you think a human body can take?

. . .

I never turn them (children's hospitals) down if it is humanly possible, not because of what I think I can do for them but because I know they will listen to me like an old friend, and I may be able to help them get well by providing an incentive or interest in life they may have lacked. It makes me feel very humble when I'm told some little guy or gal is going to get well just because they've got a date with Sheik (Tim's rodeo horse) and me. That's what rodeo means to me—a chance to get around this country of ours and get in touch with the kids who will, when their turn comes, inherit it. If I can do a little bit to help make them stronger, happier youngsters, then I'm tickled pink.

JACK HOXIE

I know a lot about the old 101 (Wild West Show). It was a great show—one of the best. I know Tom Mix and Buck Jones were on the show one year each. I was on the show four or five years. Colonel Zack Miller told me a lot about Tom Mix, Buck Jones, and Bill Pickett—the greatest bulldogger we ever had. I think I was closer to Zack than anyone on the show.

. . .

I was the first man to put the Appaloosa breed horse into

motion pictures. Zeb Hunter, who had a ranch near Lone Pine where he bred horses said, "When this colt is born and when he is one year old we will go up and get him." One day Hunter and I saddled up and rode up to where the bunch was and saw him, and he was the prettiest thing I have ever seen. He was white and had a lot of spots on him—the Appaloosa breed. When he was a year old, Ben Corbett and I roped off his old daddy, "Old Crumpy." His mother was a range mare. We brought him into Lone Pine and brought him back to the studio with the other horses. When he was four, I started riding him in my pictures.

HERB JEFFRIES

(regarding his independently produced films) We didn't have writers or stuntmen. We had nothing. I did all my own stunts, my own fight scenes, I helped write the music. I did everything but direct the pictures.

• • •

I made most of my money following the pictures around making personal appearances singing with the Four Tones on stages where these pictures played.

• • •

I decided sometime ago the Negro people need all the good, intelligent, non-belligerent representatives they can get and I try to be one.

(author's note: Jeffries was the only black B-western star.)

BUCK JONES

(regarding his start as a rodeo performer) I put resin on my chaps to help me hold the saddle and drove horseshoe nails into the heels of my boots to keep my spurs on. I then went and asked for a tryout.

• • •

(regarding his dislike for singing cowboys) They use them to save money on horses and riders and ammunition. I'm one of the old time cowboys, the sort the kids used to want to grow up to be like.

• • •

I've been hurt so many times making movies I stopped counting long ago. I've had seven fractures. I've broken my right foot, both hands and both collar bones. As if that wasn't enough, I was once almost roasted alive. A scene called for me to be soaked with gasoline and set on fire. The fire spread too fast. I started to run. Bob Perry, an ex-prizefighter, knocked me out with a punch to the jaw, wrapped me in a blanket and smothered the fire. But it pretty near killed me. I had third degree burns to the waist!

TOM KEENE

I did not want to be known solely as a cowboy. I gave up westerns, so people would forget me. I must say it is more stimulating to bring to the screen THE LOUISIANA PURCHASE for instance, than any number of nonsensical and sappy fictitious pieces in which I've appeared.

JOHN KIMBROUGH

I was contacted by 20th Century Fox for a screen test. I was tall and athletic and had good name recognition due to my college football career. They were looking for a cowboy star to replace George Montgomery, who was being moved up to a higher grade of westerns. My agent was Everett Crosby. Everett was Bing Crosby's brother. After the screen test, I was called to sign a contract. Everett told me to say nothing, but to let him negotiate for me. The studio's first offer was for $750 a week— I almost jumped out of my chair. I wanted to sign before they changed their mind. However, my agent talked them into agreeing to pay me $1,500 a week.

(author's note: Kimbrough starred in only two B-westerns, LONE STAR RANGER and SUNDOWN JIM.)

JOHN "DUSTY" KING

Actually I didn't like the man (Ray Corrigan) very well and had much rather talk about Max Terhune. Max was one of the greatest guys I ever knew.

ALLAN "ROCKY" LANE

(When asked in later life about what he had been doing) I'm old, bald and fat. I haven't done anything in years except the voice of the horse on TV in "MISTER ED."

(When interviewed very early in his career) Don't ask me whether my real name is Lane or not. I played football for several years with that name and that's the one I kept. I started with Orange (New Jersey) that year and wound up in Paterson, and when the Tornadoes disbanded I came over to the Panthers. When the movie offer came, I decided to take it and retire from football. And I intend to stay in the movies as long as they'll have me.

LASH LaRUE

I was called in for an interview by producer Bob Tansey. After a few minutes, he said to his secretary, "Well, he looks the part but can he act?" I told him, "I'm probably the best actor that's ever been in your office." He said, "He's either good or he's nuts!" Then he told me he was wanting someone who could use a whip. I told him I had been messing with one since I was a kid. I then went out and rented a couple of whips and practically beat myself to death trying to learn how to handle one. When Tansey called me back to sign a contract, I had to tell him I'd never used a whip. He said, "But you told me you'd been messing with one since you were a kid." I said to him, "Now wait a minute, Bob. You doubted I could act. So, I acted like I could use a whip." I pulled up my shirt and showed him all the welts on my back and neck. We had a good laugh about it, but he still signed me.

• • •

I met a lot of men that I hated their guts, but I never met a woman I didn't love.

• • •

(regarding his confrontation with Hugh O'Brian on the set of WYATT EARP) I wish the good Lord had let me snuff that twerp.

• • •

A few years ago, a cheap comic book company started putting out Lash LaRue comic books. I called them and asked about my royalties and they said, "We thought you were dead!"

. . .

Someone wrote that I rode like I was glued to the saddle. My producer said, "That's the only way he could stay on!"

. . .

My horse was named Black Diamond. I tried to change his name to Rush, but it didn't work. He was a quarter horse; he was great. I know if there is a heaven for horses that he is there.

. . .

I did a couple of science fiction movies during the 1980s. The scripts weren't much, but the money was American.

. . .

Everybody uses a little of Lash LaRue, here and there. But nobody sends me any money! If my residuals ever catch up with me, I'm going to buy a piece of Hollywood and burn it.

. . .

Age is a psychological trap. If I started thinking about how old I was, I wouldn't be able to get up in the morning.

. . .

Someone once asked me when I made my last movie. I told them I haven't made it yet.

. . .

I never let my family see me making movies. I didn't want to try to explain what I was doing. Maybe I really didn't know what I was doing. My mama did go to see me in SONG OF OLD WYOMING; I got killed in it. She sat there and cried like a baby.

. . .

We made my pictures in five days. They didn't waste time—or money.

. . .

Fuzzy St. John was a dear; he was an angel unaware. He drank too much. I didn't know why until I met his wife. After meeting her I understood. She was more like a keeper than a wife.

. . .

I've been around a long time and been to a lot of places and met a lot of people. Someone said it's un-American to not know Lash LaRue.

. . .

I've attended a lot of film festivals, and I'm flattered by all the attention I still get. I only wish Fuzzy was still around to see how long we've lasted, I don't know why I'm still popular. I thought I'd be dead by now.

BOB LIVINGSTON

In those days the actors had to do a lot of their own stunts. I got banged up pretty good myself. On the first day of shooting TRIGGER TRIO we were out on location for a hot moment in the film where I'm supposed to make a dive off a bridge into the Kern River. I did the stunt, but nearly tore the top of my head off on a rock at the bottom. The studio rushed in Ralph Byrd to finish the picture. And since I hadn't done any of the intimate, close-up scenes, it didn't make any difference in the production schedule.

• • •

One day Yates called me into his office and handed me the schedule of Republic pictures for the following year. I was surprised to see I was being taken out of westerns to play the lead in higher budgeted non-westerns. They were going to replace me (in The Three Mesquiteers) with John Wayne. After STAGECOACH, all anyone in town was talking about was John Wayne. So Yates called me back in again, but this time he told me John Wayne was going to get all the parts promised to me. I stuck my tongue in my cheek, thinking at the time here I am getting passed over again. But I accepted it and went back to The Three Mesquiteers for the 1939-40 season.

• • •

(regarding his relationship with Ray "Crash" Corrigan) Just say we were friendly enemies—let it go at that.

• • •

Don't give Yates (head of Republic Pictures) all the credit for the films, mine or others. It was the people in them that made them.

JOCK MAHONEY

Charlie Starrett put a lot of beans on my table. As a stuntman, I've doubled many stars, but Charlie is primarily responsible for my career—that's where I learned my trade—not only as a stuntman, but as an actor.

• • •

Andy Devine's old horse just hated Andy. Andy weighed over 300 pounds, and every time the horse saw him coming it would put up its ears and try to bite Andy. I don't blame the horse —I wouldn't want Andy on my back either.

• • •

We had some wing-ding fights where I'd completely demolish everything in sight, but good always won out. That was the message of the TV westerns. And that's something that should be on TV again.

KEN MAYNARD

(After signing with Fox, the studio decided Maynard needed a make-over) There I was, wearing a big white hat, high heel boots and spurs, riding a loaded trolley across Los Angeles; going to have the hair on my hands removed and my eyebrows plucked.

• • •

Fox was having trouble with Tom Mix and Buck Jones. They signed me on a three-month contract as a replacement, but they both quieted down and they let me go.

• • •

I've made a lot of money in the business, and have spent several fortunes foolishly I know, but I'm just a dumb cowboy, and would probably do the same things all over again.

• • •

I have always liked Gene Autry. He knew how to keep his money. That's more than the rest of us did.

KERMIT MAYNARD

No matter how good you are as a stunt man, when you become a star the studio always insists on furnishing you with a double. It's studio policy, but not in my case; I always performed my own work.

• • •

I've never approved of him drinking. You see, I don't drink. Never have. And I don't smoke. I play nine holes of golf every day I'm not working. All Ken has done for years is sit around in that trailer of his and drink.

TIM McCOY

I walked out of a contract at Monogram (The Rough Riders series) because the war was on. I used to say at the time any guy who was physically fit to do the things we had to do in western pictures ought to be in there doing his stuff. We had a war going on. And not playing Indians. So I sent them a telegram and walked right off. They said they could have had me deferred. Deferred my eye!

• • •

My lawyer advised me to never own anything that eats. I rode what the studio rented for me. I rode for work, but not for pleasure. I've never been sentimental about my horse. If you want to know the truth—horses are dumb and I want nothing to do with them.

• • •

It is gratifying that I was able through all these years to give these youngsters an example, a decent example. I'm very pleased about that. They've turned it around. They've made the image something totally different. It's the tough guy who's the hero, not the fine upstanding fellow. And then the sickness that's coming into them now. Gracious, films are filled with nothing but filth and pornography and profanity. They have to fall back on that just to give people a thrill. Well, heavens, it's no thrill to go around and listen to words you used to see written on fences.

• • •

(regarding the heavies and extras) They were a gallant group of hard-riding, hard-working cowboys. In those days of film-making, the director's main concern was for the actual picture. Many good riders and horses were crippled, maimed or killed by the orthodox methods used to obtain certain falls and spills for the benefit of the movie fans. And those poor riders didn't have any medical plans or insurance poiicies.

• • •

I had lots of fun doing them (movies). I liked the income and I liked the life and certainly never regretted having gone into pictures.

• • •

I have no regrets; I'm pretty well satisfied with what life has done to me and what it's been. There's nothing to be bitter about. There's nothing to be dissatisfied about. I've been a very fortunate man. And that sums up my life for you.

JOEL McCREA

During World War II, I refused to play a military hero. Since I was too old to be called, I was too old for that kind of show.

• • •

I've never had star rating because I dislike responsibility. A picture hangs on a star. When a picture is bad, the star is washed up. A leading man, such as I am, hangs on to a picture.

• • •

I think the picture business has become too tied up with sex, pornography and violence. Not that I'm prudish about it. I just think such things have gotten movies too far away from their primary purpose: to entertain.

• • •

I've always kind of tried to keep that western thing. I can't speak for anyone else, but that was the image I wanted to portray. I wasn't trying to prove I was the greatest actor in the world, but I tried to prove that I was legitimate and authentic in what I was doing, whether it was with horses or whatever. And I have kind of tried to maintain the integrity of that image.

TOM MIX

(regarding his retirement in the early 1930s) You're asking me if I'll go back to pictures again? I figure it this way. A fellow can't live on buttons. And that's all we were getting paid by studios a while back. So I figured if I left the studios, I had enough buttons on my britches and enough silver on Tony to let me and Mrs. Mix eat for a while yet—but I may go back. Anyway, it isn't for a lack of offers.

• • •

When a man's been married half a dozen times, any sentiment about anniversaries is as cold as the ashes of last year's campfire. Paying all them alimonies sorta drowns out the romance.

(author's note: Mix was married five times.)

• • •

(explaining his decision to return to the screen) I was mad at conditions I saw and read about each day. Criminals on the loose; boys and girls learning communist propaganda in schools; crime news filling the papers; so I figured I could help by returning to the screen in a picture which would set an example for kids to follow—one with good old fashioned virtues and western justice. When Mascot Pictures Corporation showed me the story, THE MIRACLE RIDER, I knew I had the kind of rip-sortin', he-man chapter play which would thrill every kid in town.

ROBERT MITCHUM

(regarding making Hopalong Cassidy westerns) I thought I was going to play romantic leads but the producer said I looked mean around the eyes and asked if I could ride a horse. I lied and told him I could. I got on the horse a couple times and was thrown off. I took the handle of my gun and smacked the horse across the nose. One guy on the set said, "Mister, you can't do that." I told him, "Mister, these people are paying me $50 a week to ride this horse and I'll smack him or anybody else who gets in my way."

• • •

He (William Boyd) drank more than any man I ever saw. Boyd kept quarts of whiskey on the set. He drained one every day.

• • •

I believe my film debut was in BORDER PATROL, a Hoppy picture. I made seven films with him. Supper on the ground, free lunch, a hundred dollars a week and all the horse manure you could carry home.

CLAYTON MOORE

I just never wanted to do anything else after I started the Lone Ranger. I fell in love with the character. I think playing the role made me a better person.

• • •

(regarding Jay "Tonto" Silverheels' death) I went to the hospital with his wife to see him. It was terribly heartbreaking. I leaned over the bed and said, "Jay this is Clayton. Keep fighting. We all love you." It was a terrible shock seeing him looking like that—so emaciated, such a shadow of the great man he had been. I was deeply saddened by Jay's death. We were like brothers.

• • •

The kind of contact and identification people got from The

Lone Ranger is missing. I'm for any show that fights for what is right and good. But unfortunately, we don't have very many and we need them badly.

GEORGE MONTGOMERY

I got a job on my second day in Hollywood. I found out they were looking for a bunch of riders for a scene in a Greta Garbo movie. I was a good rider, for I had ridden all my life. So on my second day in town I got work—and on a Garbo movie—I was in heaven!

AUDIE MURPHY

I'm working under a serious handicap; I have no talent. I've made the same western 40 times, only with different horses.

GEORGE O'BRIEN

When Buck Jones made his first picture at Fox, I was the assistant camera man. Buck was all man, and after his death in the Boston fire those who had worked with him felt a great loss. I was in the Aleutian Islands preparing for the invasion of Attu and Kiska Islands when I received the news.

• • •

My favorite picture was THE IRON HORSE because it was a success. It could have been an awful flop, and John Ford and I would still be trying to make a living some place. So it did two things; it gave me an opportunity and it gave Ford his opportunity, because up until that time he'd been making the little Harry Careys.

• • •

To say the least, John Ford was an inspiration to actors. Also, I think Ford, myself, and John Wayne all started from humble beginnings, and when we realized we were up against it—we went to work. And work in those days meant practically living at the studio. I slept in my dressing room many times.

• • •

You know, everyday, there's a picture in the mail box

someone has sent me to autograph, and I always do and send them back. I think that's part of being in the picture business. I'm grateful for my career—it's made it possible for me to do what I want.

DARCY O'BRIEN
(George O'Brien's son)

Growing up with my dad, George O'Brien, was great for me as he was a very attentive father and took me on trips and to ball games. I wasn't aware until later in life just how great a star he had been. He did pal around with some western people, including John Wayne, but his greatest friend was John Ford. That friendship dated from 1924 and THE IRON HORSE. Like Duke Wayne, he recognized Ford as a genius and felt indebted to him. My father was intelligent and articulate, and had a great dignity about him. He was very religious—never did miss Mass on Sunday and often attended church during the week. Unlike John Ford, he never got drunk. What you saw in the westerns was how the real George was. During his last years I had him stay with me in Tulsa, Oklahoma. He was a big hit with my friends and entertained them with stories of the old days. He was a fabulous raconteur, very Irish in that way. Until the age of 82 he was terrifically athletic. There has never been a better man than my father.

(author's note: Darcy O'Brien was not an actor, but I thought readers would like to know of his love and admiration for his father.)

DUNCAN RENALDO

I learned to ride very carefully because when I was at Republic working on those Mesquiteer pictures with Bob Livingston, a camera truck skidded into me and pushed both myself and the horse I was on through a barbed-wire fence. The horse broke two of its legs and I broke my ankle.

• • •

Allan (Lane) was not too sweet, but I got along with him fine. He used to be so damned temperamental at times and he was stubborn.

• • •

At the end of our shows, I would say to Leo Carillo, "Oh, Pancho!" and he would say, "Oh Cisco!" Then we would both laugh and ride away. I invented that little gimmick for one reason. If we both laughed at the end of the pictures, then the kids who watched us, instead of being confused, would know it was for entertainment and comedy.

• • •

The Cisco Kid never killed anybody. We tricked the bandits into killing each other off instead of our doing it. We manhandled them a lot, but we always turned them over to the sheriff.

• • •

You know, TV goes into people's homes, with little children watching, and it's mayhem. It's fearful—the death and the killings. It doesn't make sense. After 1955 in TV something happened—like a disease set in, and people began to shoot everybody. The minute they had the slightest altercation, the first thing, a gun came out, and at least five people dropped dead. The fun has gone out of it. And warped thinking has taken its place.

• • •

Leo "Pancho" Carillo could not drink. He was allergic to liquor. If he drank even a thimbleful, he'd get red in the face and break out. People used to think he was drunk, but that was because he was always in high spirits. I called it an effervescent personality. He was a wonderful man; he bubbled all the time.

TEX RITTER

I remember once my mother said it would be nice if her three boys would sing. So we got up in front of the fireplace and sang about half a song and the others stopped and said, "Mama, would you make him sit down." They didn't think much of my singing.

• • •

I wanted to be a lawyer, but after a while I had to drop out of school—I ran out of dishes to wash and had no money.

• • •

He (Al Jennings, the reformed outlaw) taught me how to handle a gun—he taught me the fast draw. I was with Al about a month when I came to Hollywood, learning my gun work. Later I would see Al Jennings around California a lot. Sometimes we'd go to softball games together.

• • •

We (Tex and Rita Hayworth) had a couple of dates, played tennis a few times, then I took her to a horse race and I recall the horse we bet on lost. I would call her house a lot after that and her father would answer, "Rita isn't in," and finally he changed it to, "She won't be in," so I always figured he must have felt a cowboy from Texas should at least be able to pick a winning horse for his lovely daughter.

• • •

It was in 1941 I found him (his horse White Flash) at Mr. Eddy's (Jerome Eddy of Chino, Arizona). He was pure white in color with perfect quarter horse conformation and the deepest black eyes you ever saw. Glen Randall trained him for me and the horse could do everything except put his hands in his pockets.

• • •

I guess I was pretty tough (in the movies). Roy and Gene sang more—I killed more. I must have killed old Charlie King at least twenty times. Usually it was behind a rock. You've got to give Charlie King credit. He was a ballet artist the way he went about it. And he was a natural comedian. He was always so surly on the screen that very few people would have guessed his comic talent.

• • •

(regarding his race for senator from Tennessee) The public remembered me as a two-gun, lead-slinging cowboy and just wouldn't take me seriously at politics. I lost out to Bill Brock, heir to the candy fortune.

• • •

I really enjoyed working with him (Bill Elliott) and he was a very likeable fellow. He rode like he was born in the saddle, although like me (and he laughed), he had a double for any dangerous stunts. He was the star, but I think we had equal time to show what we could do. I guess you have to call it a fifty-fifty set up, and we got along just fine.

ROY ROGERS

One day I walked into a little place in Glendale to get my hat cleaned and blocked. A tall good-looking fellow came running in to pick up a hat; I think his name was Carter. He was all excited about Republic looking for a new singing cowboy star. He said he was going to try to get the job. Well, I decided to try too. The next morning I headed out to the Republic Studio. I didn't even know if I could get in. I didn't get very far because the guard stopped me at the gate. I waited until the lunch crowd returned and slipped in with them. I'd only walked a few steps when I felt someone tap me on the shoulder. Well, my heart sunk because I thought it was the guard and he was going to throw me out, but it was Sol Siegel, the producer. Mr. Siegel remembered me from The Sons of the Pioneers. I told him why I was there. He said he had never thought about me for the job, but to run and get my guitar and he'd give me a try. I ran so hard to get the guitar I was out of breath and could hardly sing. I guess I did all right because on October 13, 1937, I signed a contract for $75 a week. The studio decided I needed a new name. Several of us met in Mr. Yates office. (Yates was the head of Republic.) We kicked several names around and finally the name Rogers came up. Well, I liked that name because I had always loved Will Rogers. Then someone mentioned Roy, I didn't care too much for that name because I once knew a kid named Leroy who I didn't like. When they put both names together—Roy Rogers—it sounded pretty good. So that's how I became Roy Rogers. I believe the good Lord must have wanted me to become a cowboy because of the way things worked out. If I hadn't been in the hat shop, and if I'd been ten feet behind or ahead of Sol Siegel he wouldn't have seen me. If these things had not worked out the way they did, I may have never become Roy Rogers. I'm sure glad I did because I wouldn't change a thing. The stables that furnished horses for the studios brought over several horses for me to try out. I believe Trigger was the third horse I rode. I knew right then he was the horse I wanted. I didn't even try any of the other horses. I thought he was the prettiest horse I'd ever seen and he would be perfect if I were ever lucky enough to make some color movies. After my first picture, I went to Clyde Hudkins who was the owner of Trigger and asked him if he would sell me the horse. I told Mr. Hudkins if he would sell me Trigger I would try to see to it his horses were used in all of my films. He agreed to sell me Trigger for $2,500. He told me I could pay him a little at a time. That was a lot of money for a fellow who was broke and only making $75 a week! We shook hands and Trigger was mine. Trigger was part thoroughbred and he could really fly! I think it was Smiley Burnette who suggested we call him Trigger for the phrase "Quick on the Trigger." He was a wonderful horse and was with me in all my films. When Trigger died in 1965, at the age of thirty-three, I didn't have the heart to bury him. I knew what would happen to him if I put him in the ground. I had seen what a beautiful job they did mounting animals; so I decided to have Trigger mounted. I'm mighty glad I did because now folks can still see Trigger when they visit my museum.

• • •

Mr. Yates came to me with a script he wanted me to do. I read it and found I was to play a smart-alecky Pulitzer Prize winner who drank and smoked—everything opposite of what I stood for as a cowboy. I returned the script and told him I wouldn't do it. He told me I had to because I was under contract. I still refused and was off the lot for about two weeks before Mr. Yates finally called and said he had gotten someone else to do the part.

• • •

Arlene died shortly after Dusty was born. It nearly killed me, too. But I had a family to care for. You have to do the best you know how at a time like that and just keep on going.

• • •

Dale and I were put in a position of role models for many American boys and girls, and believe me, we have taken that job seriously. I used to have a beer or two when I was off hunting or fishing, but there came a time when I realized drinking even a beer didn't fit the kind of person Roy Rogers was supposed to be. I thought about how bad it would look if someone took a picture of me with a drink in my hand, so I gave it up altogether.

• • •

One reporter wrote the only reason Roy Rogers and Dale Evans were adopting children was for publicity. I could have pinched his head off! He's probably never been to an orphanage and seen little kids without a Mom and Dad. We've had four adopted children and one foster child. It's been a long time, but if I met that reporter fellow today, I'd still poke him right in the nose.

• • •

I enjoyed making pictures, but it was just a job. The best part of my life is my family. We've had our share of hard times just like everyone else. We lost three of our kids, but we've had our good times too. I feel the good Lord has truly blessed us.

• • •

The cameraman and the crew were my strength. They were terrific. They were good friends and I loved them.

They worked extra hard to make good things happen.

• • •

I never was much for the big Hollywood parties. I'm just a homebody. I enjoy one on one, or being with my family. I appreciated the invitations, but I didn't know what to do after I got there. I just didn't speak the same language—if you know what I mean.

• • •

It seems like everybody knows Roy Rogers. I feel like I've touched the lives of a lot of wonderful people and I know they've certainly been nice to me. I think I've grown up with practically everyone that's alive today.

• • •

I always appreciated my fans and tried to treat them right. After all, where would I be without them? I visited hospitals and orphanages all the time for children. Sometimes they weren't even strong enough to shake hands, but they could always manage a smile. I tell you it really warmed my heart. I always felt a responsibility to the kids, to be somebody they could look up to.

• • •

Gene Autry and I are thirty-third degree Masons. I visited a Shriner's hospital and saw all the good those folks did for kids. I made up my mind right then I wanted to be a Mason.

• • •

Gabby Hayes was wonderful. He was like my father, my brother, and my buddy all wrapped into one. I loved him and I still miss him.

• • •

Today's movies are so filthy I wouldn't let Trigger watch them.

• • •

I'll never retire. It's like the old saying about dying with your boots on. That's the way I want to be.

• • •

(regarding his rule not to sign autographs in person) Once you start signing autographs, you can't stop. I like to shake hands and talk to people. I can't talk and sign at the same time. When I start to write, my mouth shuts. So I prayed about it and tried to think of something else to do. I decided instead of signing autographs, I would shake hands, pose for photographs, and talk to the people. I believe most folks are happy with my decision.

• • •

I've never even seen a marijuana cigarette and if that

sounds old fashioned, then I am! But as Popeye said, "I yam what I yam."

• • •

I try to always remember that I'm just an old country boy from Duck Run, Ohio, who happened to get a job in the entertainment world.

GILBERT ROLAND

(regarding his asking for dialogue changes in the Cisco Kid films) I wanted to be sure the Mexican was not portrayed as an unwashed, uneducated savage clown—I refuse roles that picture Mexicans as ridiculous, quaint or foolish.

CESAR ROMERO

The first Cisco Kid was Warner Baxter, and he won an Academy Award for playing the part in a picture called IN OLD ARIZONA. That was in 1929, and it was the first all-talking western, which caused a sensation. In my case, my first Cisco role was in THE CISCO KID AND THE LADY in 1939. I ended up doing six Cisco Kid pictures, and I loved every one of them. The Cisco Kid movies were fun because I was on a horse all the time, and I loved to ride. Also, each movie was well made with high production values.

BUDDY ROOSEVELT

I had no particular interest in being a sagebrush cowboy celebrity, but I did love the hazardous life, performances and talent in the circus, rodeo and stuntman's world.

• • •

I should have been more careful about getting my image established in only B-westerns. Such tie up contracts have been changed in the last few years by the efforts of our agents and union, giving the star more flexibility to portray different characters in both TV and big productions.

REB RUSSELL

There was one particular scene where Rebel (Russell's horse) had to act like he was looking at a photo I was holding in my hand. So the way we got this shot was we put a carrot on my knee, oh, he loved carrots, and when I called him over he would look down, see the carrot and grab it. We went through the maneuver three or four times then we didn't put a carrot there. Rebel looked down and it looked like he was looking at the picture. Bob Wills offered me $10,000 for that horse, but I wasn't about to sell him.

FRED SCOTT

Bill Boyd always fell in love with his leading lady until he married Grace Bradley. She was the saving of Bill. One day the old DeSoto broke down and I was trying to get it started. Who should come down the street but Bill Boyd. He had pistols for door handles, longhorns mounted on the front. It was really an eye catcher. He got out and helped me with that old car, and then went into the shop and met all the employees, signed autographs, etc. He was one of the most real people I ever met. Not a phony in any way.

• • •

(regarding the reported Bill Boyd's dislike for children) He certainly was affectionate with my two little girls. And, anyway, it doesn't fit his character, he was a first class, warm human being. I still miss him a great deal.

• • •

I believe very strongly that the young people should have ideals. I personally do not drink or smoke and have never used drugs. I believe we should all take care of ourselves, physically, mentally and, above all, spiritually.

• • •

Gene Autry is a kind and generous person. He has helped more people than anyone will ever know. It's common knowledge in Hollywood Gene took care of Ken Maynard in Ken's latter years. Of course, Gene doesn't tell about these things. The checks Ken received never came directly from Gene. They came from a round about way so Ken would never know they came from Gene.

• • •

Jean Carmen was a fine rider and a marvelous little actress. A few years ago, I was signing autographs at a film festival and next to me was this charming lady. I looked over and saw it was Jean. She was in her later years also, but she sure didn't look it. I dropped everything and went over and picked her up, hugged and kissed her, and said, "I've been meaning to do that for the last fifty years!" In the B-westerns, we seldom were allowed to kiss the leading ladies.

* * *

Al St. John got the name "Fuzzy" when he worked with me. The part was planned for Fuzzy Knight, but for some reason he wasn't available. The script called for my side-kick to be called Fuzzy, and they just used that name for St. John.

* * *

Old White Dust has been dead now for many years. He wasn't a great trick horse, but he was wonderful and a beautiful animal. We always doubled him in the long scenes, because we did not want him to get sweaty. When a white horse gets sweaty, it photographs gray.

* * *

Lash LaRue is one enjoyable guy—part lusty poet, half evangelist, and 100% fun.

* * *

All is serene as I try to remember we have the opportunity to emulate the trees and flowers around us, to be calm and bloom ourselves. To know that God is ever-present in this world, and it is our duty to know it, and everlastingly to affirm it. All is lovely outside my house, inside my house and within me—glory to God!

RANDOLPH SCOTT

I was advised to never let yourself be seen in public unless they pay you for it. To me that makes sense. The most fascinating star our business ever had was Garbo. Why? Because she kept herself from the public.

* * *

I never intended to become an actor, but one day I was playing golf with Howard Hughes, just after he had pro-duced HELL'S HINGES. As a lark he got me a job as an extra. Maybe it was the uniform I wore on the first day, but I decided, if one could become an officer merely by applying to the wardrobe department, I'd do the rest of my fighting in the movies.

* * *

All I can say is I enjoy my family. I play golf, I've been blessed with a good constitution and I tend to mind my own business. I'm not a good person to ask about today's movies because I don't go to them.

CAL SHRUM

In the late thirties everybody wanted to play with Gene Autry. I remember twice in about 1936 or '37 we went to Hollywood to try and get in films with Autry, but we couldn't get past the studio gate. Later while we were playing a job in Kansas City, as luck would have it, Sol Seigel, Autry's producer, came to hear us and offered us a chance to be in an upcoming film with Autry. This was our start in pictures and we appeared in many after that.

CHARLES STARRETT

My team (Dartmouth) turned down the invitation to the Rose Bowl. Johnny Mack Brown's team (Alabama) accepted the invitation and Johnny turned out to be the star of the game. Johnny was a handsome guy and was offered a movie contract. If my team had gone to the Rose Bowl, Johnny may have never become a movie star.

• • •

Cliff Edwards was a wonderful sidekick in my films. I wanted to keep him, but when it came time to renew his option he was told, "You comedians are a dime a dozen." He went over to RKO and started working for Tim Holt at twice the salary Columbia had been paying him.

• • •

Smiley Burnette and I didn't hit it off too good at first. He told me he had come over to Columbia to give my series a shot in the arm. Well, I'd been at Columbia for several years and had done all right without Smiley, so that remark did not set very well with me. Smiley worked hard and we became good friends. He was an asset to my pictures.

• • •

When Jock Mahoney started working in my films, he was all over the place. He did a lot of my fight scenes, stunts, and most of my riding. I kiddingly told some people I was only around to do Jock's dialogue. He was a tremendous athlete.

• • •

Boris "Frankenstein" Karloff and I were among the founding members of the Screen Actor's Guild. Boris loved flowers and had a beautiful flower garden. One day, as I was driving home, I stopped at his house and Boris was out watering his flowers in his Frankenstein make-up. Can you imagine Frankenstein out watering his roses?

* * *

Dick Curtis was an excellent heavy in my films. He had a great face for a heavy. We had so many fights we got the routine down to perfection. We must have made a couple of dozen films together. We tore up everything in sight, but I don't remember either one of us ever getting hurt. I used to slip into the theater showing one of my movies and really get a kick out of the kids whooping and hollering when they saw me and old Dick mixing it up on the screen.

* * *

The Durango Kid was not my favorite role. Who wants to make pictures with their face covered up? I did enjoy the Durangos, but I had rather have made movies without the mask.

* * *

I wanted to call my horse Yucca. It's a type of cactus, you know. The studio wouldn't let me because they said nobody would know what it meant. We finally decided on the name Raider.

* * *

My family isn't the least bit impressed with my career and my neighbors think I'm one of them—a retired businessman.

* * *

I'm positive a TV series based on the old westerns—with plenty of fast action, thrills and suspense—would give today's kids a whole new crop of heroes—American kids today need heroes to respect and look up to.

* * *

I agreed to do this Robin Hood, I call it, this Durango Kid series. I did that for five years. I did about fifty or sixty of them. And you know, after the first ten it was like doing the same story over again. But that's what they liked. If I'd have said no, they would have fought me, and I would have lost out. You were like a ball player, and you did what the manager said.

BOB STEELE

I toured the country with Black Jack O'Shea. At every little theater, we put on a fight demonstration for the fans. Old Jack was a pretty mean guy on the screen, but in real life he was one of the nicest fellows you ever met. I think he settled down and ran an antique shop.

• • •

I never went in for all this hoop-de-do about being an actor and demanding high salaries.

• • •

I do love westerns. The outdoor life appeals to me and they are good, clean entertainment for young and old alike.
I made a picture with Clint Walker. I never saw such a big man! I rode horses smaller than he is.

FRED THOMSON

(regarding his leaving the Presbyterian ministry) The movies gave me a wider scope in that they reached thousands instead of just a few hundred. They appeal to the younger generation, who perhaps do not go to church, and yet are most in need of guidance.

• • •

(regarding performing his own stunts) It is all a matter of mathematical calculation. These daredevils who depend on chance take risks. But I don't. I figure out weights, distances and such things.

(author's note: He must have miscalculated when a stage ran over his leg and broke it during the filming of THUNDERING HOOFS.)

TOM TYLER

(when his agent asked him if he could ride) I said, "Yes"— and didn't even gulp! I knew if there was a way to stick on, I'd find it.

• • •

(regarding his role of Buffalo Bill in the serial, BATTLING WITH BUFFALO BILL) It was a wonderful part. I love the out-of-doors and the feeling of a good horse under me will always be a thrill, but that doesn't make me unfit for anything but cowboy portrayals.

JIMMY WAKELY

Monogram was a place where stars were born and stars went out of the scene. You got your break there because they couldn't afford much money. So, they would get beginners and those that had gone over the hill would come there to make movies because they couldn't get jobs at the big studios. I came to Monogram to get going, and fellows like Johnny Mack Brown went there to die.

• • •

My first picture, SONG OF THE RANGE, came out in 1944. Within sixty days it was in the black. So the studio decided to drop the Cisco Kid series and continue my pictures. I was there for five years and made twenty-eight movies. (When accused of copying Gene Autry) Everybody reminds somebody of someone else until they are somebody. And I had rather be compared to Gene Autry than anyone else. Through the grace of God and Gene Autry, I got a career.

• • •

A lot of people said that Smiley Burnette "made" the Autry films. Smiley was good, but you could take Gabby Hayes or someone else, and as long as you had Gene Autry you still had the best going. Smiley wasn't successful with everybody. He wasn't very good with Bob Livingston, Sunset Carson and Eddie Dew, and Republic let him go.

• • •

Lee "Lasses" White was getting old and the studio was too cheap to double him in the riding scenes. He was a good rider but he was so old I was afraid he would get hurt. I finally asked him to quit and we replaced him with Dub Taylor. Lasses was a Mason and he lived it to the hilt. He had friends all over. He was a wonderful person; I just loved the man.

• • •

The production manager wanted to cut down on my songs and take me out of my fancy clothes. I told him I was not an actor and he would ruin my career.

• • •

He (Tex Ritter) was a generous, kind and thoughtful man who made everyone feel important.

• • •

There's the Bible, and there is wrong and right in all of us. If, through the media of motion pictures and television we can be stripped of the children's respect for the family circle, if we can be stripped of our belief in a Supreme Being or a hereafter, if we can be stripped of our heritage, of our belief in our country and any right things we might have done, if we can be stripped of our historical values, if they can get us to where we don't believe in anything, this whole country will fall apart like a bag of cookies. If we make a youngster think that everybody's rotten, that everybody's bums, they go out and rob a filling station. But, you make him believe in a Supreme Being and a hereafter, and he has good moral conscience to adhere to, then his conscience will keep him straight.

JAMES WARREN

Those Zane Grey pictures were not B pictures. They used top camera crews. Our still camera man had won an Academy Award for still pictures. We had one shot, the last shot of the day up in Lone Pine, where the mountains were in the background and the sun was behind the horse and its flowing mane looked like it was on fire. Just beautiful photography. I want to put that in as these were real class "A" pictures—I enjoyed the time making westerns and I'd like to do it all over again.

JOHN WAYNE

Being called Marion made me the target for every bully in town. They called me, little girl; asked why my mother dressed me in pants instead of skirts; did everything they could to make my life miserable. At the age of eleven, I got a paper route. I would stop by the fire hall with my Airdale, "Little Duke." The fireman started calling me "Big Duke." You can't imagine what that meant to me. When they began calling me "Duke", I made up my mind to use the name from now on.

• • •

Nobody liked my acting but the public.

• • •

Anybody who would make an X-rated movie ought to have to take his daughter to see it.

• • •

Planes, cars, trains are okay for speed, but for excitement, there's nothing like a horse.

• • •

I play John Wayne in every part regardless of the character, and I've been doing okay, haven't I?

WHIP WILSON

To know Andy Clyde out of character was the surprise of a lifetime. He was a very proper English-Scots gentleman and spoke very proper English. You never just dropped by his home. You needed an invitation. Andy had a special room in his home no one was allowed in. The room contained mirrors and props so he could constantly rehearse his character.

WHEN A COWBOY FAILS
by Bobby J. Copeland

Our hero seemed so perfect when he rode the silver screen. All his deeds were admirable and his character squeaky clean.

He captured our hearts and fantasies and he taught us the way to go; but in real life he often failed us, and it really hurt us so.

Though his image may now be tarnished, let us be slow to condemn. Remember, except for God's grace, it could be us instead of him.

Pardners, we never rode in that cowboy's saddle, or saw the world through his eyes. We never felt his heartbreak or heard his mournful cries.

Some became cheats and liars, and others could only fail. Some became drunks and paupers, and others went to jail.

Some of their souls were blackened, and others gave up on life. Some forsook their children, and others more than one wife.

Some tried their level best to bring honor to God's name, while others enjoyed long lives and found fortune, favor. and fame.

Perhaps some reached for righteousness, only to fail miserably. Perhaps others searched for satisfaction, but ended up like you and me.

But none of them were perfect; no, not a single one. Perfection was attained only, by God's beloved Son.

So let's forget where they failed us, and hold them in our hearts; and always cherish the memories they left us, when they played their cowboy parts.

Section II

SIDEKICKS

Next to his horse and six-shooter, the B-western cowboy hero's best friend was his faithful sidekick who rode with him on every exciting adventure. While the sidekick was along to provide companionship and laughs, one of his primary purposes was to communicate the hero's intentions to the movie audience so they could be aware of the his next move. After all, there was a limit to how much a cowboy could talk to his horse. The sidekick occasionally provided musical interludes, assisted the hero in his many battles to combat evil, and often rescued the hero from the romantic notions of the ranchers' daughter.

Gabby Hayes is the favorite sidekick of most western film fans. However, the overall success of the comic sidekick can be traced to Smiley Burnette. In 1935, Burnette was teamed with Gene Autry. The pair became an instant favorite with movie fans, and Burnette's large role and his wide range of comic antics paved the way for the many sidekicks that followed.

ROSCOE ATES

I was a bad stutterer for a long time. I finally was able to cure myself by practicing my talking in front of a mirror. When I got into pictures, I thought it would add humor if I stuttered on some of my words. It turned out to be pretty funny, but the P.T.A. complained and I had to stop. I only stuttered occasionally in the pictures after that.

SLIM ANDREWS

I couldn't ride very well when they signed me to work with Tex Ritter, so they gave me a mule to ride. Well, that son-of-a-gun had been used as a cutting horse and could really run. There was times that it would outrun Tex's horse, White Flash.

• • •

I had a good scene with Smiley Burnette in one of Gene Autry's pictures. I thought it turned out pretty funny. When it was over Smiley said, "Hey Bud, you're funny, but you won't be in any more of Autry's pictures; I'm the comedian around here." Smiley knew what he was talking about because I never made any more movies with Autry. Smiley was in good with Autry.

• • •

I don't think Tom Keene ever said a word to me. I worked in those movies with him and we did our lines and that was it. I don't mean that he was mean or temperamental, he just wasn't a talker.

• • •

Don Barry was temperamental. He was a little guy and didn't like it when I was put in his pictures. He wouldn't do a scene with me unless he was sitting down or I was sitting down.

• • •

One day Glenn Strange and his band stopped at my house to spend the night. After supper, my wife started to clean off the table. Glenn said, "Now wait a minute! After a good meal like this, we sure ain't gonna let this little lady wash the dishes." So Glenn and one of his boys did the dishes. Now that was a sight—big old Glenn Strange in an apron washing dishes.

• • •

I worked with a lot of stars, but Tex Ritter was the best. He was always honest, easy-going, and he was well-liked by everyone. If you had Tex for a friend, you had a friend for life. Tex was my friend until he died and I sure do miss him. It was Tex who got me started in the picture business.

BOBBY "LITTLE BEAVER" BLAKE

My father hated my success. He wanted to be there instead of me, and if not him, then the apple of his eye— my brother. But it was me.

PAT BRADY

I've been very lucky. I joined The Sons of the Pioneers after Roy Rogers signed with Republic. We did several films with Charlie Starrett over at Columbia before moving over with Roy. After the war, I was out of the Pioneers and worked in Roy's films and TV show as a comic. You couldn't work with finer people than Roy and Dale. Later on I got the chance to join back up with The Sons of the Pioneers. Yes sir, I've been mighty lucky.

SMILEY BURNETTE

I was working on this little radio station in Tuscola, Illinois, when one day I received a phone call. The caller said, "This is Gene Autry." I said, "Sure it is, and I'm General Grant." After convincing me it really was Gene Autry, he asked me, "How much are you making at the radio station?" I told him they were paying me $18 a week. He said, "I need an accordion player; I'll give you $35 a week. Think it over and let me know. I said, "I've done thunk it over; I'll take it."

PAT BUTTRAM

They say Columbus discovered America in 1492. Iron Eyes Cody says it was never lost in the first place.

• • •

I didn't get along too well with horses. You know, those things are hard in the middle and dangerous at both ends.

• • •

Bob Livingston was in the first picture I made with Autry. I thought he was the best looking actor in the movies.

• • •

Gene Autry used to ride off into the sunset; now he owns it.

• • •

Gene was always a horse trader. When he signed an autograph for a little girl, he saw dollar signs instead of curls. I remember he used to sell a Gene Autry songbook over the radio for 50 cents. Then he'd come in on Saturday and pick up his mail. He'd sit in front of the wastebasket, shake each envelope so the coins would slide down to one corner, and then hit it on the rim of the wastebasket. the envelope would break open, the money would fall out and he'd hand the envelope to his secretary. I'll always remember that wastebasket half filled with silver.

TOMMY COOK

Don Barry was very good to me, as were the rest of the crew of ADVENTURES OF RED RYDER. I read for the part of Little Beaver along with other boys. And, of course, I look like an Indian. All they had to do was throw a wig on me. I also did Little Beaver on radio for something like four and-a-half years.

ANDY DEVINE

I never had any acting lessons. I just played myself—an Arizona hayseed.

• • •

I made a deal with my sons years ago. If they'd do nothing to embarrass me, I'd do nothing to embarrass them. It's worked out fine.

BUDDY EBSEN

I did a few westerns with Rex Allen. We had a lot of laughs. He'd call me by my first name, Christian, and I'd call him by his, Elvie.

• • •

When I was working with Fess Parker in Davy Crockett, I

never had to worry about a double chin. Fess was one actor I always looked up to.(Ebsen is 6-foot-3, but Parker is 6-foot-5.)

RAYMOND HATTON

I enjoyed my work with Johnny (Mack Brown). My agent convinced me to leave the series. He claimed he could get me bigger pictures and more money. I did pretty good but I still missed working with Johnny.

• • •

One of the saddest moments in my life was when I learned of the tragic death of my good friend, Buck Jones. Buck was a credit to the picture business and was loved by everyone. Buck, Tim (McCoy) and myself had some good times making the Rough Rider pictures.

GABBY HAYES

A movie studio owner named Trem Carr saw me in my false beard in my theater act and asked me to grow a real one for the six-day movies he was making with John Wayne and Bob Steele. I shaved it only once since then—in 1939, when I had four months off. But my housekeeper saw me without my beard and was scared to death. I looked in the mirror, and it sure scared me too. I never shaved it again.

• • •

The pictures I most enjoyed acting in were TALL IN THE SADDLE with John Wayne and Ella Raines, and THE RETURN OF THE BAD MEN with Randy Scott. They were quality westerns, and that Ella sure was a pretty one. I liked working for Cecil B. DeMille, too. I was pretty fidgety because I heard he was a tough director. But he turned out to be real understanding and I was able to give a performance that pleased my fans.

• • •

I've always said my act is a small-town character from New York State, which is where I came from, with a western accent. Of course, the kids won't believe I'm an actor, and I think they're about right.

STERLING HOLLOWAY

I didn't care for my role as Autry's sidekick, and I really didn't care for horses. Horses and I had a mutual agreement—they hated me and I hated them. I was glad when the Autry pictures were over and I could get back to roles for which I was more suited.

CHUBBY JOHNSON

It's too much trouble to tell a lie. If you lie, you got to remember the story. If you tell the truth, you don't.

RICHARD "CHITO" MARTIN

Many people think I'm Spanish and speak with a Spanish accent, but I don't. I played with Mexican kids when I was growing up. I learned to speak their dialect by mocking them. We had a lot of fun—they would mock me and I would mock them. Many of the things you learn as a kid stick with you. Learning the accent proved beneficial to me in the "Chito" role.

• • •

Tim Holt was a wonderful friend. He was kind and giving— never selfish. Tim would sometimes skip his raise—have the studio give it to me. How many people do you know who would do that? Tim was a good actor and a splendid horseman. We remained friends but didn't see much of each other after the series. Tim moved to Oklahoma and I stayed in California and got into the insurance business.

• • •

Those quick dismounts from the horses caused terrific wear on your knees. I've had both of mine operated on. I'd just as soon played something else other than a cowboy.

FRANK MITCHELL

When I was hired to work with Bill Elliott and Tex Ritter, they brought me a beautiful white stallion to ride. I thought it was a little strange they would provide me with such a beautiful horse. I climbed aboard and took off right in front of the whole crew. About that time, someone started playing a record of the "Star Spangled Banner." When the horse heard that music, it reared up and started pawing the air and doing all kinds of shenanigans. I had to hang on for dear life. The horse had been a circus performer and had been trained to act up when that song was played. I'll never forget that experience.

• • •

I replaced Dub Taylor in the Elliott/Ritter series—Dub had been called Cannonball. So, the studio just decided to call me Cannonball too. Bill and Tex were wonderful guys to work with. There was no jealousy between them, but I'm sure they would have been happier having their own series.

SLIM PICKENS

I know I'll never be an actor, but let them (the directors) find that out for themselves.

• • •

My father was against rodeoing and told me he didn't want to see my name on the entry lists ever again. So this rodeo guy said to use another name. "Why don't you use Slim Pickens, 'cause that's what it's going to be." My name was Louis Bert Lindley Jr., and I figured it improved my moniker.

• • •

They're not making many (westerns) right now, but all it takes is just one good one and they'll come back like "gangbusters." The western is the closest thing to a fairy tale that we have in this country. It's our heritage. A lot of people still love westerns.

SNUB POLLARD

I guess I was better at slinging pies than lead. In one role I was to stick up a guy, and I charged in with my gun drawn. The director nearly had a fit. Guess I wasn't holding the shooting iron right. The kids are the best audiences. You can't fool them, but they're your most loyal fans. They'll go anywhere to see you.

AL (FUZZY) ST. JOHN

I've been around pictures a long time and worked with a lot of good cowboys. I had fun and they treated me swell. I guess I enjoyed working with Buster (Crabbe) the most. We worked well together and he appreciated me. I think we had about equal screen time and made about the same amount of money. When Buster left the series, they brought in Lash LaRue. Lash and I got along just fine. We made a lot of personal appearances together.
(regarding the potential success of one of his films) No way of telling. It's sorta like an unborn baby. You don't know if it's a boy or girl until it's born. With films, you never know until it comes out of the cutting room and goes on the screen.

JAY "TONTO" SILVERHEELS

When I was a kid, I hated the Indians in the movies. They were always so cruel. I hated the Indians before I realized I was one myself. That shows how badly the films were slanted. I am proud of my ancestors, too, because they were here to greet your ancestors.

DUB TAYLOR

Bill Elliott was a wonderful fellow to work with. I got the name Cannonball while working with Bill. I don't know how they came up with the name. I guess it was because I was kinda round and short.

MAX TERHUNE

(regarding the success of the Three Mesquiteer series) I thought it was because it offered something for everybody. For the girls, it had a running gag of rivalry between Stony and Tucson in each story. It had plenty of action and fights and the boys liked that. I like to believe the kids liked Elmer too. And the adults, I think, liked the variety of plots and scenery and the beautiful horses. A lot of credit has to go to Yakima Canutt. He directed the action and the fights— and not only directed but performed in the horsefalls, wagon turnovers, climbing and water stunts.

• • •

I loved every moment of it (making westerns) and have many wonderful memories. I have had the opportunity of working with some of the most talented people on earth.

EDDY WALLER

I got along all right with Rocky Lane. If someone met with misfortune, Lane would give him his last dollar. He was always compassionate.

LEE "LASSES" WHITE

I used to drink, but I wouldn't walk up and hit Jack Dempsey; he'd knock me on my backside. Whiskey is also able to knock me down. Anything that can knock me down, I can't take.

CHILL WILLS

I did some pictures with George O'Brien. Now George was a nice fellow, but one day he came up and put his arm around me and said, "Chill, you're going to go a long way in pictures, but you ain't going to be in no more of mine."

Section III

HEAVIES & HELPERS

The actors who portrayed heavies—or badmen—were usually a despicable lot, who spent their time rustling, raiding, robbing and performing other dastardly deeds. There were three type of heavies: the boss or dress heavy, the action or dog heavy and the henchman heavy. The boss heavy provided the brains and was usually a well-dressed business man held in high esteem by the unsuspecting townspeople. He planned evil capers and instructed his cohorts in carrying out crimes while remaining in the background. Often, it was near the film's end before he was identified as the main culprit and had to face the hero and pay his dues.

The action heavy supplied most of the brawn. This desperado carried out the orders of the boss heavy. He was the one challenging the hero to a brawl and after losing (he always did), he devised murderous schemes to get rid of the hero. Many times his role was larger than that of the boss heavy and often he would be killed off before the hero's confrontation with the boss heavy.

The henchman heavies constituted a group that rode with the action heavy. They were brainless and unsightly individuals who blindly supported the action heavy. They had few lines and little to do except look mean and to throw lead and fists.

The helpers were generally youthful performers who sometimes rode along with the hero and his sidekick, and often assisted them in their never ending battle to "clean-up" the old west.

Others helpers were fathers, good businessmen, uncles, livery stablemen, musicians, ranchers, juveniles, good townspeople and those in various other supporting roles.

CHRIS ALCAIDE

He (a director at Columbia) asked me to come in and read for a part of a heavy in a western (SMOKEY CANYON). We did that in one week. Every time you see the Durango Kid in the black mask it was Jock Mahoney doubling for Charles Starrett, and he also played another part in the picture. I was bulldogged off a horse twice and did three fights on my first day on the set.

ROY BARCROFT

Buck Jones truly was a man's man. His co-operative attitude toward his fellow actors was unparalleled. Buck would go out of his way to help someone. On one occasion while filming one of the Rough Riders, I developed a severe cold. Buck told me to stay in bed and he would double for me in the day's shooting schedule, which called for much action. Buck too had a tough assignment that day but he did both parts without any complaints. This is why most of the cast cried freely when we viewed the final cut of his last film, shortly after his death.

• • •

After making a picture with Don Barry, my little nephew would hardly speak to me. He said, "How could you do it uncle Roy? How could you let a little squirt like Don Barry whip you in a fight?"

• • •

Rocky Lane and I got along okay. Rocky insisted his fight scenes look realistic. One day he kept on about my performance. I got mad and popped him right on the chin and asked him if that was realistic enough.

• • •

I worked in the serial, KING OF THE TEXAS RANGERS, with Sammy Baugh. He was a great football player and had never been on a set before. He was the first lead in a serial that we could really say, "He could ride." He was raised on a ranch and had horses; his whole family could ride like rodeo kings.

• • •

It was just a job (making westerns). You'd wear the same clothes, say almost the same lines week in and week out. Don't forget also we didn't film in sequence, so often it was just one fight or chase after another.

• • •

(When he and Kenne Duncan were approached by Ed Wood, director of infamously bad films, about a possible picture) We've seen your flicks. Maybe we ain't doing too well these days, but we ain't ready for professional suicide.

GREGG BARTON

I've been knocked on my rear by every western star, including Annie Oakley. When the price is right, I'll let anyone knock me down.

HANK BELL

I've seen a lot of real good riders in my many years in this business but I'll have to give the nod to Ken Maynard. Now that fellow, when he first began making pictures could do about anything on top, sideways, and under a horse—and at a full gallop mind you! That horse of his, Tarzan, was about one of the smartest critters that ever rode in films.

• • •

If horses was dollars, Autry could ride.

NOAH BEERY JR.

Buck Jones was one of the finest men I ever knew and a fine actor. He was especially kind to the newcomers on his pictures and his loss was a great, sad event.

(author's note: At one time, Beery was Jones' son-in-law).

• • •

I have to say John (Wayne) was a man's man. He was blessed with character and persona that men looked up to and women simply adored. John was a real star—what you saw was what you got. No false Hollywood airs. Beans and coffee or red wine and steak—ranch hands or studio high brows; John was at home wherever he was.

MONTE BLUE

(regarding his return to films after being a star in silent pictures) I looked in the mirror and saw I was no Little Lord

Fauntleroy. I decided to build my new career on rock instead of sand. So I started out at the bottom as an extra. I was in the awkward stage between stardom and character parts.

WARD BOND

For years, people would look at me and say "There's something familiar about your face; don't I know you from somewhere?" I'd tell them they'd probably seen me in pictures and they'd say,"Oh, yeah, you're the fella who's always in those John Wayne movies." With the success of WAGON TRAIN, I finally became known on my own.

WALTER BRENNAN

I did several "little" westerns with people like Tom Mix and Tim McCoy. Later, I made "big" westerns with actors like Gary Cooper and John Wayne. I didn't care what kind of pictures I was making. Heck, I never wanted anything out of this business except a good living. Never wanted to be a star, or a glamorous figure. Just wanted to be good at what I was doing.

• • •

I'd rather do television than movies because there aren't any long layoffs between working days. You make a movie and then wait around for another good part. Not in television. You go to work five days a week for most of the year. That's what I like. By Sunday night I can hardly wait to get started on Monday morning. It's a shame most people don't feel the same way about their jobs.

• • •

Boy, let me tell you, there's no risque stuff on my show (THE GUNS OF WILL SONNET). No sir, I won't allow it. In a TV series, you're going right into the living room, and families are watching you. It sure burns me up to see some of the stuff they let get by on other shows.

STEVE BRODIE

I loved making those pictures with Tim Holt. I particularly enjoyed playing a bad guy. When people booed you and hated you for the role you played, it meant you had done your job well.

FRED BURNS

(Tom) Mix and (Buck) Jones were good riders, but Ken Maynard was a real daredevil, a good rider and a real good athlete to boot.

RAND BROOKS

Andy Clyde was the finest gentleman I ever knew in my life. He was like a father to me. He was a high Mason and lived it to the hilt. I never became a Mason myself, but I think it would have made Andy happy if I would have joined.

• • •

Andy was a great horseman. Of course, he was always doubled when there was a chance he might get injured. He was doubled by Clem Fuller.

YAKIMA CANUTT

I told Herbert Yates I didn't want to work any more with Rocky Lane. Yates persuaded me to continue and told me if I had any more trouble with Rocky to tell him to see the boss. Everything was fine for a couple of days; then Rocky was back to his old self. I told him if he didn't like what I was doing to see the old man. He came back in about thirty minutes like a dog with his tail between his legs. That's the last time I had any trouble with Mr. Lane. He was a poor rider; he ruined four good horses.

• • •

I was doubling Harry Carey in THE DEVIL HORSE. I was to grab Rex (a horse) around the neck and hold on to him. He couldn't shake me off so he fell on me—knocking me unconscious and breaking several ribs. I spent quite some time in the hospital over that. Rex was the meanest horse I ever saw.

GEORGE CHESEBRO

The picture business is where a guy you think is your best friend, will knife you in the back. Then, he'll call the police and they'll have you arrested for having a concealed weapon on you.

• • •

(when told he and his cohorts looked like a sorry bunch of outlaws) You ain't seen no outlaws, buddy, until you've seen my in-laws.

ROBERT CLARKE

I guess westerns were especially appealing to me because when I was a kid in Oklahoma, Tom Mix, Buck Jones, and others that I saw on the movie screen were my heroes. To my way of looking at it, they were real cowboys. Although Gene Autry and Roy Rogers were extremely successful, they, to me, did not embody the "real cowboy" as much as the Buck Jones/Tom Mix type cowboy actor. And Tim Holt fit in more with that type. He was a realistic cowboy on the screen; he made you believe he was *really* a cowboy.

EDMUND COBB

Many years ago, one of the theaters was showing one of my starring silent films. I went down to see it. When I got back home, I went and looked in the mirror and asked myself, "Where did it go (his good looks)?"

IRON EYES CODY

I think we should respect people of all nationalities and preach brotherhood throughout the world. The finest man I ever worked with in the picture business was Tim McCoy. He was a great gentleman, and he understood Indians.

TRIS COFFIN

Johnny Mack Brown was one of the nicest guys in the

entire world. He liked everybody and everybody liked him.

• • •

Rocky Lane was a practically impossible guy. He was so egotistic, so impressed with himself, and he gave the impression that nobody else had any ability or talent .

• • •

I have a photographic mind. I used to win bets lots of times. A person would take a book and open up a page and hand it to me. I'd read a paragraph and hand it back to him and repeat every word.

• • •

After Buck Jones' death, they were going to continue the Rough Riders series and set them up a little different with Tim McCoy, Raymond Hatton and myself. About that time my draft number came up, so I was in the service for a little over three years.

(author's note: Tris Coffin is apparently mistaken because McCoy had already quit the series for the army prior to Buck Jones' death.)

JUNIOR COGHLAN

Bill Boyd only had one child from his marriages—a son who died at the tender age of nine months. This was from Bill's second marriage to actress Ruth Miller. As I look back on our films together, I now feel Bill always treated me like the son he still wished he had. I truly adored the man.

DON CURTIS

(regarding his first western, TAKE ME BACK TO OKLA-HOMA) The song, "You Are My Sunshine" was first introduced in that picture; I'll never forget the Sunday morning when we shot up at Idlewild, and all of us knew that song would be a great hit. Tex (Ritter) was salt of the earth; he acted like a star sometimes, but was most personable and friendly. As the years unfolded I got to know him apart from the motion pictures, and found him and and his lovely wife beautiful people.

• • •

I wasn't interested in being a stuntman; I was interested in being an actor, but I'd do stunts. The stuntmen didn't like that much, and they made it pretty rough for an actor who took their jobs away from them. I don't blame them. So, I got ridden off a few times; a guy would uncork one in a studio fight once in awhile.

JOHN DOUCETTE

I enjoyed working with him (Tim Holt), and found him to be a gentleman. I also worked with his father (Jack) once at Warner Brothers. I didn't realize it prior to working with Tim, but he was as great a horseman as his father was.

JOHN DUNCAN

When I was growing up back in Missouri, my dad had a barber shop next door to a drug store. I used to buy cherry-phosphate sodas there and the soda-jerk was Bill Elliott. One day he came by all dressed up and told us he was going to Hollywood and try to become a motion picture actor. Some years later, I was making a film on the lot next to where Bill was shooting. I went over and introduced myself as the kid who liked cherry-phosphate sodas. We had a good laugh about that.

(author's note: In addition to his other films, John Duncan played Robin in the 1949 serial, BATMAN AND ROBIN.)

KENNE DUNCAN

Everybody wondered what a football player (Sammy Baugh) would be able to do in a western. But you should have seen him handle a horse. He could take direction well too, and he learned a lot about acting quickly. If he had stayed in the business, he could have been as big as John Wayne.

GENE EVANS

My first film was a Monte Hale western (UNDER COLORADO SKIES). Pictures used to be built on characterization, and the stories tied these characters and their relationship together, that was the success of the earlier day westerns. Even on my first picture they had some good actors like Paul Hurst. He was right at the end of his career; but when I went on and saw him, I thought, "I can't believe it; that man's a big star." I'd seen him do some masterful things in movies. Monte was a great big farm boy, and he just kind of plowed through this with a big grin on his face; that's all he was required to do, and sing a song and strum a guitar.

TOMMY FARRELL

I worked with Andy Clyde in the Whip Wilson series. He was a great guy and a wonderful comedian. In real life, he was much different that he was in front of the camera. He was serious, quiet, and very dignified. Andy was an intelligent man who read all the time.

JACK ELAM

I remember Ben Johnson when he was young and handsome. Now look at him—he's damn near as ugly as I am.

TERRY FROST

Charlie King was a great guy, but he was an alcoholic. He tried to kill himself twice. One time he shot himself with a twenty-two, and another time he climbed a tree and tried to hang himself. Either the limb broke or the rope broke and Charlie ended up with a broken leg.

• • •

I used to call Allan Lane,"Mother" Lane. He was always fussing about something. He didn't like anyone and nobody liked him. I didn't work much with Lane and that suited mc just fine.

• • •

I worked with a lot of the singing cowboys including Gene Autry, Roy Rogers, Jimmy Wakely and Eddie Dean. To me, Eddie was the best singer of them all; he had a beautiful voice and he's a heck of a nice guy.

• • •

Whip Wilson was the clumsiest cowboy I ever worked with. They started the Whip Wilson series because of Lash

LaRue. I worked in several pictures with Whip. A real nice guy, but he couldn't act his way out of a paper bag.

• • •

I thought Monogram made the best westerns—story-wise, for one thing, and the directors.

DON HAGGERTY

Many, many things you look back on, and I will say I thoroughly enjoyed the westerns more than anything. It's more freedom and you're out of doors. The guys are all fine—a nice bunch of people.

DON HARVEY

One of our better known he-man western stars is in for a big surprise on his next picture. The booted "gentleman" has had a lot of fun actually slugging the movie "heavies" he always whips in "reel" fights. He has broken two noses to date. What he doesn't know is that his own studio has arranged to have an honest-to-goodness pug meet him in his next screen slug-fest. The studio is tired of paying damage suits and the pug has orders to cure the hero, once and for all. This we want to see!

(author note: Although not identified, Harvey is probably talking about Rocky Lane.)

• • •

Shug Fisher, one of The Sons of the Pioneers, says it is easy to figure your own cost of living. "Simply take the total of your earnings and add 20 percent!"

• • •

Advice to parents from Clark Gable: "Give pig and a boy everything they want. You'll get a good pig and a bad boy."

• • •

We liked the statement by Roy Rogers: "No matter what other nations may say about us, immigration is still the sincerest form of flattery."

MYRON HEALEY

He (Dennis Moore) was never what you'd call a team

player. I don't know whether he didn't like the business or was just a private man.

BEN JOHNSON

I may not be a good actor, but nobody plays Ben Johnson better than Ben Johnson. Riding a horse is not easy; it's kind of like dancing; it's all in keeping rhythm with the horse.

• • •

John Ford was miserable to work for, but he was my education in the business. He thought he could scare you and get a better performance. I wasn't smart enough to be scared and I told him a time or two what he could do with his old movie.

• • •

As long as people make me a living, I've got time to sign autographs. When I'm tired and can't sign I get out of sight. Actors who don't appreciate the fans enough to sign autographs didn't get the right kind of milk when they were growing up.

• • •

The reason they don't make good westerns these days is because the new bunch of directors don't know one end of the horse from the other—and they won't listen to people that do.

I. STANFORD JOLLEY

Only in quiet, personal conversation with Buck (Jones) could one find and feel the rich, mellow tones of his voice. It is needless to say, the entire crews involved in the many productions Buck starred in loved this wonderful man.

DICK JONES

I came to California from Texas at the age of four with western legend Hoot Gibson. To me, western life is as natural as breathing. We need westerns today where the bad guys are bad and the good guys are good and the worst four letter word is whoa!

• • •

Buck Jones was one of the finest men I ever knew. I've worked with many cowboy stars but his is the only photograph I have hanging in my house. I wish I could have made more pictures with Buck Jones.

• • •

The first day on the set of THE RANGE RIDER, Jock Mahoney suggested we do all of our own stunts. So after the first day, Jocko and I did everything our characters were seen doing, no matter how dangerous. Believe me, I still feel some of the lumps. Today, I wouldn't get within a hundred miles of a horse.

• • •

Hollywood just stopped making the rah-rah, shoot-'em-up, good-guys-wear-white-bad guys-wear-black westerns. Instead, they started making a whole bunch of psychological westerns like GUNSMOKE and MAVERICK, and people forgot about our Saturday morning shows.

VICTOR JORY

(regarding the arrival of police after a fight with a drunken Big Boy Williams) They said, "You're both under arrest for fighting." I said, "We're not fighting; we're just having a little rough and tumble fun." I guess Big Boy liked that. The police said, Well, go to bed and stop all of this." Big Boy said, "You're all right, Victor." He took hold of my pajamas and when he pulled his hand away, I had no pajamas. He said, "Let's have a drink." I had a quart of gin in my room. We went into my room with no door (it had been broken down in the fight) and he poured me a drink in a small glass and poured the rest into a pitcher. While I drank the glass, he drank the water pitcher.

BILL KENNEDY

I worked in a western with Johnny Mack Brown. Johnny was a wonderful guy. He didn't give a damn about who got the best close-ups; he didn't care about those things. A wonderful guy, a good poker player, and everybody loved him. Unfortunately, he didn't save his money and it was a sad ending. Later on he was a greeter at a very well known place out in the valley, called Cock of the Walk, a very posh restaurant. You'd call him up and reserve a table. I called

Roy Rogers and Dale Evans with the author at the 1989 Roy Rogers festival in Portsmouth, Ohio. Roy and Dale delighted the fans when they made one of their rare festival appearances. Starting in 1943, Roy was voted the no. 1 money-making western star. He continued to top the poll until it was discontinued in 1954.

Hank Worden — John Wayne took a real liking to Hank and cast him in many of his films through the years. He is shown here during the Charlotte, North Carolina Western Film Fair in 1987.

(Photo by Tom Wyatt)

Eddie Dean and Lash LaRue with the author at the 1985 Charlotte, North Carolina, festival. Eddie was the first B-western star to make color features. He and Lash attended many film festivals. Eddie said he was proud that Lash got his start in the Eddie Dean series.

Buck Taylor and his father Dub "Cannonball" Taylor with the author at the 1986 Knoxville festival. Buck Taylor played the role of Newley on TV's GUNSMOKE. He has worked in several A-westerns, TV, and he is a professional artist. Dub Taylor was the comic sidekick to several cowboy stars including Bill Elliott, Charles Starrett and Jimmy Wakley. After the demise of B-westerns, he continued to work in movies, television and commercials.

Fred Scott and fan Gary Kramer at the Charlotte film gathering in 1983. Scott made a series of westerns for Spectrum in the late 1930s. He had an opera trained voice and was billed as the "Silvery-voiced buckaroo." Scott was a fine gentleman and greatly appreciated his fans.

(Photo by Grady Franklin)

Directors Thomas Carr and R. G. Springsteen with the author at the 1987 Knoxville, Tennessee, festival. Carr and Springsteen turned out some great action westerns for Republic. Carr directed several of the Sunset Carson features, and Springsteen was the director for many of the Red Ryder films.

Rex Allen and daughter Bonita with Bob Lassiter (deceased) at the 1985 Atlanta, Georgia, festival. Allen made 19 starring features for Republic. He was the last B-western star under contract to that studio. Allen rode one of the most beautiful horses in the movies, Koko. After his starring days and after completing his TV series, FRONTIER DOCTOR, Allen narrated many of Walt Disney's outdoor features. *(Photo by Tom Wyatt)*

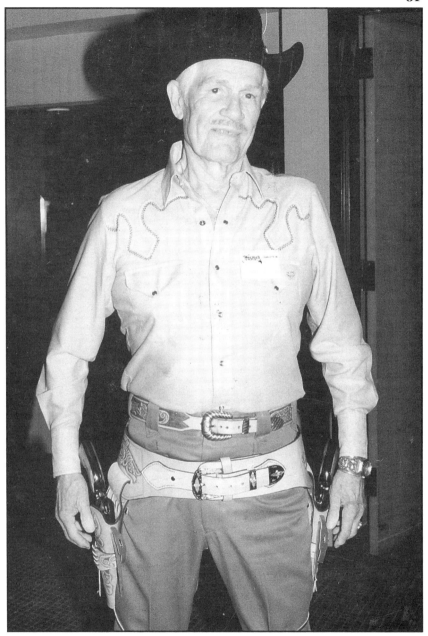

Pierce Lyden poses for Tom Wyatt's camera at the Charlotte, North Carolina, Film Fair in 1987. Lyden has appeared at many film conventions and although almost always a bad man in B-westerns, in real life he is one of the nicest gentlemen that anyone could hope to meet. Beginning in the mid-1930s, Lyden worked with practically all the B-western stars.

Left to right: John, Laura, Rebekah and Bill Black with Charles Starrett in Raleigh, North Carolina, in 1985. Starrett made all of his 131 western films for Columbia. In over half of these films he portrayed a character called The Durango Kid. This very popular star passed away in 1986.

The author with Jimmy Ellison at the 1991 Charlotte Festival. Ellison is best remembered for his role as Johnny Nelson in the early Hopalong Cassidy pictures. In 1950 he and another former member of the Hoppy crew, Russell "Lucky" Hayden, teamed for six features for Lippert studio.

At the 1982 Charlotte Film Fair, Marie Windsor and George Montgomery renewed their acquaintance and recalled their Hollywood acting days. Miss Windsor was born in Marysvale, Utah, on December 11, 1922. Montgomery was married for nearly 17 years to Dinah Shore. He is one of 14 children of an immigrant Russian farmer. *(Photo by Tom Wyatt)*

Screen favorite Bob Livingston signs a poster for a fan at the 1985 Atlanta festival. Livingston is best known for his role as Stony Brook in 29 of the Three Mesquiteer films. His brother, Jack Randall, also made a series of B-westerns. Livingston passed away on March 7, 1988.

(Photo by Tom Wyatt)

Bobby and Joan Copeland with Sunset Carson at the 1986 Knoxville fan gathering. Carson's 15 features for Republic rate as some of the most action-filled B-westerns ever made. Sunset was one of the most popular stars to ever appear at the western film conventions. Carson died of a heart attack in 1990. He is buried at Jackson, Tennessee.

Clayton Moore at Memphis, Tennessee, in 1983. Moore worked in many westerns and serials, but he will always be remembered for his role as TV's THE LONE RANGER. Due to a legal battle, he was temporarily restrained from wearing the famous Lone Ranger mask.

(Photo by Tom Wyatt)

The author with Virginia Vale at the Knoxville Festival in 1993. Miss Vale worked in films at RKO with George O'Brien and Tim Holt. She also made several musical shorts with Ray Whitley and his Six Bar Cowboys. Vale retired from films in the early 1940s.

House Peters, Jr. and Evelyn Finley at Charlotte in 1988. Peters worked in many western and non-western films. He later had a starring role in TV's LASSIE. Finley got roles in many westerns due to her riding skills. She could perform many daring stunts and she doubled many of Hollywood's leading ladies including Elizabeth Taylor, Donna Reed, Judy Garland, Kim Novak, Gale Storm and Olivia de Havilland.

"Arkansas Slim" Andrews with the author at the 1986 Asheville, North Carolina, Festival. It was Tex Ritter who suggested to Andrews that he try the movies. Andrews appeared in several films with Ritter and later toured the country with him. Andrews' last role as a comic sidekick was with Clayton Moore in the 1952 film, BUFFALO BILL IN TOMA-HAWK COUNTRY.

Ben Johnson, Ray Whitley and fan George Ashewell (deceased) beamed for the camera at a 1976 Florida Film Festival. Ben Johnson worked in many western films and is regarded as one of Hollywood's finest horsemen. He won an Academy Award as best supporting actor for his performance in the 1971 film, THE LAST PICTURE SHOW. Ray Whitley appeared in many westerns primarily as a musician. He made a series of musical shorts for RKO in the 1940s. Whitley once managed The Sons of the Pioneers, and he wrote "Back in the Saddle Again" for Gene Autry. *(Photo by Don Key)*

John Duncan, the author and Lyle Talbot at the 1990 Knoxville festival. Duncan appeared in a few westerns, but he is best remembered for his role as Robin in the 1949 serial, BATMAN AND ROBIN. Lyle Talbot had a long and distinguished career in both films and TV. He was one of the founders of the Screen Actor's Guild.

Bob Allen starred in B-westerns in the mid-1930s. He and Charles Starrett attended Dartmouth University and both made westerns for Columbia. *(Photo by Tom Wyatt)*

Kay Aldridge was loved by all when she wowed the fans who met her at the Knoxville show in 1987. *(Photo by Tom Wyatt)*

B-western heroines Carolina Cotton (left) and Lois Hall delighted the audience at the 1989 Knoxville Festival.

Yakima and Andrea Canutt at the 1984 Western Film Fair held in Raleigh. Canutt pioneered stunting in western films. He starred in a series of silent films, and later was a character actor in many western films. He directed the chariot scene for BEN HUR. In 1966 he was awarded a special Oscar for his contributions to the stunt profession and for developing most of the safety devices still in use by stuntmen today.

John Hart with long time fan Janet Foushee at Milo Holt's Western Film Club meeting in 1990. Also pictured is Sammy Fulp dressed as Tonto and leading a horse resembling the Lone Ranger's famous Silver. During Clayton Moore's contract dispute, Hart starred in several TV episodes of THE LONE RANGER. *(Photo by Don Key)*

Monte and Joanne Hale flash big smiles for the camera of fan Howard Moore at one of the Memphis, Tennessee Film Festivals. Hale made 19 features for Republic (some in color). In his films he rode a horse named Pardner. Hale's big grin and Texas drawl made him an instant hit with all the film fans.

him and he recognized me right away, which I was thrilled over that. This is after I left Hollywood and had gone back to Detroit, and he hadn't seen me in twenty years. But my God, he remembered my name on the phone and I was thrilled to death. I went out there, and he gave me a fine table and we talked for awhile. He looked good; he was kind of heavy but he still had that wonderful drawl and a little boy look about him that he never lost. I appreciated him taking care of me, I was with friends and they were very impressed. That was a big thrill.

• • •

I worked with Whip Wilson. He was a very friendly and down to earth guy, but he could never handle that whip. He was pretty clumsy and there were some hilarious scenes involving him and that whip of his.

HARRY LAUTER

You never met a nicer guy than Roy Barcroft, and he was a fine actor. I'm sure he would have gone on to greater things if he hadn't gotten typed as a western heavy.

• • •

I used to really enjoy dressing up. One day I came to the set all decked out and Marty Robbins was there. He saw me and said he was going to write a song about me—and by gosh he did! He wrote one of his biggest hits, "A White Sport Coat and a Pink Carnation."

MARC LAWRENCE

I only recall, while under contract to Columbia, a tall, rather modest personality in Charles Starrett. I must have played a not very pleasant character.

• • •

Gene Autry created the name, *Gene Autry*, as a commodity way before Marlboro Cigarettes or Coca Cola got the idea. He was clever enough, and to his credit, to always use Gene Autry in every character he played in every film he made.

• • •

Don (Barry) worked in some of the TV episodes I made. I enjoyed Don's wonderful enthusiasm for living. Later, he fell in love with a young girl and his zest for life suddenly ended by suicide.

GEORGE J. LEWIS

He (Whip Wilson) was pretty good with that whip. I remember one scene with him, I was playing the heavy, pulled my gun out and started to fire. He snapped that whip and curled it around that gun and got it right out of my hand.

TOM LONDON

I don't know how many pictures I've been in. I know it's over 2000. It's like asking how many pairs of socks you've worn in your life. If you put on socks every day for fifty years, that's a lot of socks. Well, I've been in movies for more than fifty years, and that's a lot of pictures.

• • •

I got along with all of them, with the exception of one. I especially liked Wild Bill Elliott, and though a lot of people found Rocky Lane too hard to work with because he was too much of a perfectionist...I enjoyed working with him on around 12 pictures and respected that he tried to make his films stand-out over the usual little western. One of my favorites to work with was Sunset Carson. He encouraged me with giving me his "sidekick" roles in his pictures that paved the way for future roles. A star I owe a lot to was Gene Autry. I made around 18 pictures with him and he was one of the nicest guys to work with. He always saw that I got decent characters to play, and in RIDERS IN THE SKY, I got a great part playing a cowpoke in a big death scene. I've been told that this was the best acting of my whole career. Later on when I auditioned for some television work, I would bring along a 16mm print with that scene and show it on a casting agent's office wall and most of the time I got the part. I made six pictures with one of the highest paid stars. Ken Maynard, who was a real SOB to reckon with...many times he was "liquored-up," mean as hell to everyone on the location and especially with his horses. Later on, I turned down work in his pictures.

PIERCE LYDEN

(author's note: Pierce Lyden worked in many western films. I have asked him to comment about the stars with whom he worked.)

(Johnny Mack Brown) Johnny was a real friend. He was one of the best gun twirlers and fastest draws in Hollywood. I got to be pretty good, but not as good as Johnny. I was in a lot of Johnny's films.

• • •

(Tex Ritter) Tex, like Johnny Mack Brown, was a good gun twirler, horseman and actor. He was a great fellow to work with. He was a big man and certainly looked like a cowboy.

• • •

(Jimmy Wakely) To my way of thinking, Jimmy Wakely did not fit the bill as a western star. Jimmy always had trouble in the fight scenes, and was not a good horseman. He wasn't the rough and tough kind of person. He was a gentle man, more interested in being a good singer than a cowboy star.

• • •

(Clayton Moore) I worked with Clay many times. He was one of the most professional actors I have had the pleasure to work with. He was serious and a gentleman, not a drinking carouser.

• • •

(George Houston) Another gentleman I remember quite fondly is George Houston. He had been a fine opera singer before coming to Hollywood. He starred in a series of pictures for a small independent studio called PRC. George died of a heart attack in 1944.

• • •

(John Wayne) He was a real man's man. Wayne was easy to work with and he worked hard. He was patient and pleasant. He became a member of the Masonic Order in 1970 and is one of the few Masons to have a lodge named in his honor. The members of the John Wayne Lodge in Metaire, Louisiana, wear western clothes to their meetings.

• • •

(Bill Elliott) Bill was another good friend. He was one of the finest persons you ever met. He really cared for people. He was liked and respected by everyone who knew him.

• • •

(Roy Rogers) Roy and Dale were everyone's friends. They hosted the Hollywood Christian Group for many years. I attended many of the meetings. A lot of the movie people were converted to Christianity because of the Hollywood Christian Group.

• • •

(Gene Autry) I began working with Gene when he switched over to Columbia Pictures. Gene Autry was a big star, but he wasn't big-headed. He was always nice and easy to work with. I think everyone enjoyed working in his pictures.

• • •

(William "Hoppy" Boyd) Bill Boyd was probably the poorest rider of all the movie cowboys. Ted Wells doubled for Hoppy. Ted was an excellent rider and looked enough like Hoppy when he put on the Hoppy suit he could ride right past the camera and you couldn't tell it wasn't Bill Boyd. Bill could barely stay on a horse when he first began the Hoppy series, but he got to do pretty good after a while—he sure looked good decked out in that black suit on that beautiful white stallion. One night my wife, young son and I went to a studio party after one of Boyd's pictures. I asked Boyd to pose with my wife and son and Topper. He said in a half-whisper, "I never get any closer to a horse than I have to." It was a disappointment to my son.

• • •

(Don Barry) Don was a temperamental little cowboy, and quite sensitive about his size. He was a good actor. I got along with him just fine. He said he was going to stay in the movies until he got an Oscar, but he never did. Sadly, Don took his own life.

• • •

(Russell "Lucky" Hayden) Lucky liked everyone and everyone liked him. He was a real friendly guy with a big heart. He never turned down anyone who asked for a handout.

• • •

(Bob Steele) I worked with Bob when he was a member of The Three Mesquiteers, and with him and Hoot Gibson in The Trail Blazers when he replaced Ken Maynard. Bob was a great little guy.

• • •

(Sunset Carson) Sunset was always fun, irresponsible, happy and fun to be around. But I don't think he ever grew-up—as Peggy Stewart says, "He needed mothering."

• • •

(Charles Starrett) I worked on several of Starrett's, but

never got to know him. I did meet my good friend Jock Mahoney there. I worked with Jock in three serials for Columbia. Jock was a great stuntman.

• • •

(Rocky Lane) I never criticized Rocky like a lot of people did—for his meticulous, fastidious and maybe pompous ways. He was looking out for and attending for himself, his job and his clothes. After all, he was the star!

• • •

(rating the stars' riding skills) First of all Bill Boyd was the worst of the lot, I give him a two; with Wakely a close second—a three; Rocky Lane—five; Dale Robertson—six; Gene Autry, Johnny Mack, Russell Hayden, Clayton Moore—all sevens; Roy Rogers, Joel McCrea, Sunset Carson and Bill Elliott—all eights. If they are not a ten, it's because they didn't have to perform, and I don't think they could have, like the old stars who did their own stunts. The tens, to me, are Art Acord, Tom Mix, Buck Jones, Ken and Kermit Maynard.

BARTON MacLANE

I don't think it's my face—at least I don't think I look like a heel. I suppose the real reason I was originally cast as a villain is because I'm a big man. You'll notice that villains are usually brawny, a fact which explains the slang term "the heavy."

SAMMY McKIM

I was in THE LONE RANGER serial and didn't even have to try out for the part. I was called in and given the script. I believe I was in the last five chapters. Lee Powell (who ended up being the Lone Ranger) was a quiet sort of fellow—not extroverted, but friendly. I liked him a lot. It was sad that his life ended as a fighting marine during World War II.

• • •

I worked on some of the Three Mesquiteer pictures. I never noticed any friction between Ray Corrigan and Bob Livingston. Many have said there was friction, perhaps I was just too young to notice. Anyway, they were both nice to me.

• • •

On one of the Mesquiteer pictures, Jack Kirk was doubling for Max Terhune. He was tearing across the landscape and was to be shot and fall from his galloping horse. When Jack took the fall he knocked the breath out of himself. The first aid doc took Jack behind a rock to revive him with a fifth of whiskey. The other cowboys kidded Jack and asked him how many nips he got from the bottle. Jack asked, "What bottle?" The doc had used the bottle himself!

• • •

Gene Autry was a quiet but likeable guy, not aggressive. We got along fine on the set. Smiley Burnette was more aggressive in his own manner, always so full of fun.

MONTIE MONTANA

I bought another pinto named Apache who had been trained for movie star Bob Baker. Baker had lost his series and wanted to sell the horse who was lame in one of his front legs. I took a chance and paid $250 for him and nursed him back to health.

• • •

Rex Allen once told me he put Koko in an elevator and someone pushed the button. The doors closed suddenly and down went the horse alone. Rex had to run down the stairs to catch him. When the elevator door opened on the ground floor, two elderly women went to get on and out walked Koko. One of the women fainted! Rex caught the horse just as he was going out the front door.

BOB NOLAN

At first you see and hear nothing, then the desert becomes alive with things few people ever see. The desert and prairie country's first impact on me was an entirely new phase of life. You see, I was brought up in the backwoods of Canada, and after World War I, I came to Tucson, Arizona, right from the tall timber, out to the desert. It was awe-inspiring, to say the least, to wake up in the morning to see the desert beauty, with the sun shining through millions of drops of dew; it was outstanding.

(author's note: The desert was the inspiration for many of Nolan's great western songs. Nolan's ashes were scat-

tered over the desert that he so dearly loved.)

BRADLEY PAGE

I was with Buck (Jones) in two films; I remember one because I enjoyed watching him twirl, he learned to twirl a lariat very well and do tricks.

• • •

Although I made several westerns, I do not like horses and never rode them. I would mount and dismount and that's all because they have riders who earn a living doing that, so I see no earthly reason some silly actor has to prove his bravery.

HOUSE PETERS, JR.

As a kid, fresh out of high school, I went to work on the Flash Gordon serial at Universal. Buster Crabbe, I and a bunch of stuntmen were working on the back lot in the 25,000 gallon water tank doing some fight scenes under the water which were filmed through large glass windows. One of them was cracked and propped up with 2 x 4s. The day after, it blew out—had we been in there at the time we would have been cut to pieces. Lucky for all of us.

• • •

I worked with a lot of great stuntmen: Yakima Canutt, Dave Sharpe, Bob Woodward, etc. I probably owe my life to Bob—he stopped a two-up team before I was run down after I had been given a falling horse to ride who did his trick fall in front of Bob's team coming along at full speed.

• • •

Please bear in mind, of my 250 appearances, only half were actually in westerns.—the balance consisting of ministers, sheriffs, detectives, and playing commercial and industrial films. I never reached the heights in the business that I wanted—never quite able to step out of my father's shadow. Closest big part perhaps was the original LASSIE television series when I played the the up-to-date sheriff for a number of years alongside Jan Clayton and George Cleveland. But I must say I had a wonderful time and met a lot of great people.

BILL PHIPPS

I've never forgotten Tim's (Holt) comments (regarding Phipps' riding ability) because they meant a lot to me. He was very curious that I could ride horses well. Well, I'm from Indiana and grew up in a rural community where I had a pony when I was a kid, so I learned to ride before I ever saw a saddle. It was second nature to me.

DENVER PYLE

I'm afraid most of the great storytellers have left us, and our business has fallen into the hands of young men that measure a picture's greatness by the size of the budget, and whose background in literature is limited to comic books. If you don't believe this read the list of titles released in the past two years.

MARSHALL REED

It was all set for me to take over the Red Ryder role when Bill Elliott was moved up. Bill and I had talked to Yates and I was supposed to get the job. At the time this was happening, Allan Lane was working on the lot in a hockey picture. Yates looked at the dailies one day and just like that, he decided Lane was going to be the new Red Ryder. Herb Yates was the kind of man who could change his mind at the drop of a hat.

• • •

Rocky was the perfect name for Rocky Lane. He was like stone. He was not one of the nice guys. He was a lousy rider and ruined two great horses.

WALTER REED

I really enjoyed making the films with Tim Holt. He was a wonderful guy and a good actor. Richard Martin and I remained friends. Those Holt pictures made a lot of money for RKO.

• • •

I really worked at my craft. There was a group of us who worked a lot—like Harry Lauter, Myron Healey, Lane

Bradford, Dick Curtis and myself. We worked a lot of westerns because they could count on us—that was the thing. It's like anything else—you have to do your apprenticeship if you want to be good.

JIMMY ROGERS

I've heard a lot of things about Bill Boyd. I can only tell you the way I see Bill. No one could have been nicer and no one could have been more helpful to me than Bill Boyd. Bill was a fine actor. He was a true professional with much experience. He did everything he could to help me. I liked him as a person, and I admired him as an actor.

• • •

Ted Wells was a darn good fellow. He doubled Bill Boyd in the Hopalong Cassidy series I did with him. He could imitate Boyd in every way—how he walked and how he rode. Those who watched the pictures didn't know the difference.

DAVID SHARPE

When Yak (Canutt) and I and the others were in our heyday we never had a worry in the world because there were so many major and little B shows. We'd work one day on a picture like STAGECOACH and then turn right around and work for Monogram or Mascot on a little five-day western. We'd do gags (stunts) for Sam Katzman at Columbia or on the back lot at Republic that would cost MGM five times as much. But half a loaf is better than none, so we'd do things for little fellows and give them a break. This meant any time I had a few days off I'd call one of these guys and I was hired immediately for whatever western or serial they had going.

• • •

If I was working at Monogram or Republic and MGM gave me a call, it was perfectly all right for me to substitute one of my fellows (stuntmen) and everyone knew he would be a perfect alternative—the right size, the correct performance. Even when I had a contract, there was no argument—they knew I'd make it up to them.

• • •

We worked very fast and did so many stunts in one day, I can't remember the details. On a western serial like

ADVENTURES OF RED RYDER, I might do a couple of flying W's, three bulldogs and four horsefalls before lunch.

• • •

It was tradition never to to discuss work with outsiders. The studios wanted the kids to think the cowboy star was doing all his owns stunts and fights. If I was doubling a star and we were both in the same costume, I avoided being near him away from the set.

• • •

I've had my share of cuts and bruises. But I have never broken anything that put me in the hospital.

GLENN STRANGE

I asked this country girl to go to a Saturday night dance with me. She talked just like Festus Haggen (from TV's GUNSMOKE). She said, "I can't go with you-all t' the dance. I can't 'cause my maw said that any man with a cauliflower ear was a roughy-tuffy."

• • •

Don't let me hear that kind of talk about stars not doing anything for others when they're at the top. My experiences are exactly the opposite.

TOM STEELE

I was called in for a screen test for the lead in a series of western pictures. I was practically promised the job, but my agent called and said the studio had chosen George Duryea; you know him as Tom Keene. His family were theater people and had a lot of pull.

• • •

Roy Barcroft was a big lovable guy, so pleasant, so easy, so real. He was a pro and always knew his lines. When I had dialogue, I had rather do it with Roy than anyone else.

• • •

I doubled Jack Randall at Monogram. Jack is a good example of what can happen when a director tries to get someone to do what a stuntman is supposed to do. Jack was killed doing a riding scene that should have been done by a stuntman.

LYLE TALBOT

(When asked if he enjoyed making westerns) Yeah, but I'm a lousy horseman, though; horses hate me. Horses are stupid but one thing: they can tell the minute you approach them that "I got a greenhorn here; I'm really going to let him have it!" You sit on them and they wouldn't move until the clappers, and then they take off. Oh, another thing was I had this back injury and I couldn't mount. They used to say you got to drop a little rope ladder for me, or mount on the high side of a hill or from a porch, just step off the porch into the stirrup. Otherwise I had to be pre-mounted or I'd play the banker in the little wagon—that was great. So I was the only pre-mounted cowboy.

• • •

Now it's prohibition, and the only guy that had any real booze on the train was Tom Mix. Tom wouldn't drink anybody's but his own; he had to know that it was real.

TEX TERRY

When I first started working in moving pictures, I think my second western was with William S. Hart. It was near the end of his career. I did stunts for a long time. I'd get $2.50 a day for rides and falls or fights. If we'd get up to $7.50 a day we'd think we were great actors at work for a big future.

• • •

I worked quite a bit with Sunset Carson. He was just a big overgrown kid out to have fun. I liked him a lot.

ANTHONY WARDE

I made westerns, but I lost a lot of work in westerns because I didn't ride horses for years. I would get on and off one so it looked like I was a rider. I wasn't interested in riding and wanted nothing to do with horses. Frankly, I was afraid of them. I guess that's why I made so many serials where cars were used instead of horses.

DAN WHITE

Lasses (Lee White) and singer Ray Whitley were in some

of the Tim Holt pictures for RKO in the early 1940s. I don't think Lasses ever had an evil thought about anyone in his life.

HANK WORDEN

When I got to Hollywood I worked in several pictures as Tex Ritter's comic relief. In some of the early pictures I went under the name of Heber Snow. That's the name I used when I was rodeoing up in Mormon country.

• • •

Tex Ritter's westerns were cheaply made. They were called B-pictures. Usually there was only one take and you had to get it right because they did not have much money. John Wayne's westerns were A-pictures. In those films they kept shooting until they got exactly what they wanted. They had plenty to spend on those pictures. You never met two finer men than Tex Ritter and Duke Wayne.

BOB WILKIE

I was born in Cincinnati Ohio, on May 18, 1914. When I came to Hollywood in 1935, I was a stuntman. I gradually worked up to better things. I was in many pictures and did a lot of TV, but I guess my favorite role was in HIGH NOON.

TEX WILLIAMS

My real name is Sollie Paul Williams. When I first started entertaining, I called myself Jack Williams. Anything but Sollie Paul!

• • •

I went to work in the early 1940s for Spade Cooley. Spade was hard to work for because he required every ounce of your energy and your companionship. Spade was never a mean man, but he required the best you had and he could get it out of you. Spade was a modest drinker on the stage, but at parties he would get bottled up. Spade and I didn't get along too good and he finally fired me. It was Spade who really launched me into show business. I will have to give credit where credit is due. I believe joining Spade was the turning point in my career.

Section IV

HEROINES

The B-western heroine usually had little to do except stand around and beautify the scenery—or to get into trouble so the cowboy hero could prove his gallantry by riding to her rescue. The heroines often had limited dialogue and received little screen recognition. Dale Evans, the most famous western film heroine of all, once exclaimed, "Even Trigger gets better billing than I do."

Strangely enough, due to their appearances at the Western Film Festivals, several of the cowgirls now have greater name recognition than they did when they were making the pictures.

While some of the women were quite good actresses, others bordered on pathetic and it was suspected they were only in the films because they were a relative or friend of one of the studio executives.

All in all, the B-western heroine's life was a pretty sorry lot. They received little money, praise or fame—and, in the movies, they seldom succeeded in getting a kiss or the cowboy hero to the altar.

Despite their limited success in the movie industry, the B-western heroine's efforts are appreciated by everyone who has a love for these grand old films.

JANE "PONI" ADAMS

Kirby (Grant) was like all the western stars I worked with—a very nice outdoorsy, down-to-earth man. Not temperamental at all. I took riding lessons for two or three days of the week. When it came time to shoot the picture I had a double and didn't get to use any of my riding experience! On one of the pictures with Kirby, I fell off into the mud—and it held up production. They had to get me—and the costume—cleaned.

JULIE ADAMS

I played in westerns until I felt ill at ease to be seen on Hollywood Boulevard without a bustle.

• • •

(regarding her six films with Russell Hayden and Jimmy Ellison) We had six different scripts—but we shot all the scenes of the stagecoach together, then all of the ranch scenes, whatever—all at the same time. I had three or four wardrobe changes—a farmhouse dress, a stagecoach dress. These films were the reason I learned to ride. Before I started, I practiced riding for about three weeks in Griffith Park.

KAY ALDRIDGE

Allan Lane was pretty—and he knew it—if you know what I mean. Allan was handsome, but he was too stuck on himself.

LINA BASQUETTE

Buck Jones was the most perfect gentleman I knew or worked with. The entire film industry respected him thoroughly.

MADGE BELLAMY

Because of the long three months in Nevada where we worked in rain and snow making THE IRON HORSE, I got to know him (George O'Brien) better than most actors I worked with. He was totally dedicated to doing his best. Looking out the train where we lived while making the picture, I could see George every morning jogging and doing calisthenics. He inherited his genial, natural rapport with people from his famous father, who was the police chief of San Francisco for many years. Everyone loved George and I was overwhelmed at working with about the most handsome man I had ever seen.

ADRIAN BOOTH

I made a picture with John Wayne called RED RIVER RANGE. John was wonderful to me. He knew I didn't know how to get on a horse and he helped me a lot with my riding.

• • •

My studio (Republic) wanted to try out Monte Hale because he was a very nice young man. He would help me with my riding and I would help him with his acting.

• • •

Monte Hale was shy in front of the camera, but he was wonderful on personal appearances. He just loved people. He started smiling and those big dimples got deeper and deeper and the crowds adored him.

RENO BROWNE

When he (Whip Wilson) was hired, my boss asked me to go riding with Whip to check him out. The horse ran away on poor Whip, but after that incident, he improved quite a bit.

• • •

When I made the Johnny Mack Brown films, they changed my name to Blair to avoid any confusion. They changed Johnny's horse's name from Reno to Rebel. Without those changes, things would have been really confused.

• • •

I have been married twice, but never had children. I was married to Lash LaRue and Lash's children by a previous marriage still call me Mom.

• • •

I was an excellent rider and could do anything on a horse the studio wanted. I did not need a double.

OLIVE CAREY

Did you know Harry Carey (her husband) never learned to drive a car? I had to drive him to the set every day and to any place he needed to go. He couldn't learn to shift gears. I can still hear him grinding those gears.

• • •

He (producer Nat Levine) was the kind of man who worked best when he was right there, while they were shooting, making the picture. Once when Harry was doing THE VANISHING LEGION, one of the actors needed a business suit. He'd forgotten to bring one with him. The scene had to be shot. Nat jumped into a rain barrel, took off his pin stripe, and gave it to the actor.

JEAN CARMEN

The studio changed my name to Julia Thayer for the serial THE PAINTED STALLION. Although I was doubled some in the picture, I really didn't need a double because I was a good rider. I made pictures with Bob Steele and Fred Scott and they both complimented me on my riding ability.

PHYLLIS COATES

I was a lousy rider. I only got on a horse when I had to and I got off as soon as I could.

VIVIAN COE (AUSTIN)

He (Don Barry) had such a temper! He would walk off the set—often stopping production just because he disagreed with Bill Witney, or somebody, about some minor thing. I don't like saying negative things about the departed, but he wasn't a very nice fellow when we worked together.

LOIS COLLIER

Horses scared me; they still do. I hated them. When we'd be on location, I'd look around and Bob Steele would have made his horse stand directly over my head, as if it were going to kick me. He thought it was funny. I didn't, as those creatures frighten me.

CAROLINA COTTON

I'll tell my name if Gail (Davis) will tell hers. My name is Helen Hagstrom. I can't tell you a lot about Gene Autry. Gail knows him a lot better than I do. I did enjoy my westerns. I liked working with Charles Starrett, but I liked working with Gene better because I had bigger parts. I didn't get into pictures because I was an actress; it was because I was a singer.

LOUISE CURRIE

He (Tim Holt) was excellent. He was a better horseman (than Charles Starrett) and I feel, an awfully good western star. He was a little bit more agile and quick. So was Bob Steele, who was also a superb western star.

• • •

All these western stars were completely different in their physical types and personalities. All were well versed in their western types. Of course Gene Autry and Eddie Dean were both singing stars in special types of westerns. I enjoyed working with all of them. The parts I played with Kirby Grant and Tim Holt appealed to me particularly. In GUNTOWN I used a bullwhip, drove a buckboard and saved the hero! So it was a very unusual role. In most westerns the girl swings on the garden gate waiting to see the hero. In DUDE COWBOY with Tim Holt I played the "other" girl, a flirt. My part was fun to play and also a little different from the typical westerns.

GAIL DAVIS

I was born Betty Jean Grayson, and then I married a Davis. So my name was Betty Davis when I signed with MGM. Well, Hollywood already had a Bette Davis, of course. The studio didn't want my maiden name because of Kathryn Grayson. So they came up with the name Gail and I've been Gail Davis ever since.

• • •

I enjoyed the role of Annie Oakley. I guess I'll be known as Annie Oakley until the day I die. The role of Annie was a natural for me because I had been riding and shooting since I was a kid.

• • •

I worked with many of the cowboy stars including Roy Rogers, Rocky Lane, Monte Hale and Jimmy Wakely, but most of my pictures were done at Columbia with Gene Autry. I did 14 films with Gene. Gene was a great boss and everyone loved working with him. It was like one big happy family. Being on location was so much fun. We bunked three to a room. Everybody ate together, slept together, and played together. Those times were some of the greatest experiences of my life.

They ran a contest throughout the United States on who should be the one to do the series (Annie Oakley). I had gone in and asked them if I couldn't get an interview for it, and they said, "Gail, you have done so many features with Autry that you were too well known as his leading lady." So I went home, put on some blue denim jeans, and a gingham shirt, put my hair in pigtails, no make-up, put freckles on my nose with a pencil, put on a pair of cowboy boots and walked into the producer and said, "Mandy, I'd like a chance to test for the part." He said, "I guess we owe you at least that," and so I tested. They were looking for somebody who could ride, shoot, act and look seventeen. I guess I made it, so I was very fortunate on that score and that's where Annie started.

• • •

I went on several rodeos with Gene. I had to do all my own shooting and riding as far as the rodeos were concerned. We even went on a tour of England where I was billed as "Gail of the Golden West." Gene took Champion, his whole crew, and all the entertainers, and it was a wonderful experience. He was a fantastic man to work for.

• • •

My last role was the skeet-shooter in the ANDY GRIFFITH TV show. I believe everyone in America has seen it. I was so type-cast as Annie that no one would touch me. They told me to dye my hair black and get rid of my accent and then come back and see us. I told them to forget it!

MYRNA DELL

On the first day of the picture (RAIDERS OF RED GAP), I was supposed to get on a horse. I went to Bob Livingston and whispered, "Which side of the horse am I supposed to get up on?" I knew enough to know there was a right and wrong side but not which was which. Bob helped me and didn't snitch on me. I've always been grateful about that. In those days, you'd get a lead in a B-western and that would be your training. They'd pay you a hundred dollars and it would take a week to do it.

ANN DORAN

It was a job (making RIO GRANDE in 1939). Nothing unpleasant happened on it—but then nothing pleasant did, either. Charles Starrett was very tall and good-looking; we got along fine.

PENNY EDWARDS

My first name is Millicent, but because of the "cent" at the end of my name, I have been called "Penny" all my life.

• • •

I enjoyed doing the westerns, but I didn't want to do serials. I was scheduled to be in ZOMBIES OF THE STRATO-SPHERE, but I begged out of it.

DALE EVANS

I had an affidavit from my parents assuring me that I was born Frances Octavia Smith on October 31, 1912, in Uvalde, Texas. Imagine my surprise when in 1954 I wrote for a copy of my birth certificate and it came back saying I was born Lucille Wood Smith on October 30. I figured my mother knew best, so, for the record, Frances Octavia Smith it will be.

• • •

(after marrying Roy Rogers) One day Cheryl (Roy's daughter) came in and said, "I wish you didn't smoke. My mother never smoked." I put the cigarette out and threw the pack in the trash basket. I quit, cold turkey, that very day.

• • •

(Regarding Roy's decision to have Trigger stuffed) Roy Jr. and I protested saying Trigger deserved a nice funeral and a beautiful headstone in a fine pet cemetery. Roy replied, "He's my horse and he'll be in my museum." I retorted, "Okay, but when you die, I'm going to put you on him." To which he replied, "Just make sure I'm smiling."

DOROTHY FAY

I worked with Lee Powell. He was a nice man. He kept to himself and didn't say or socialize much, but he was nice. I think he would have been a big cowboy star if he had not been killed in the war. Of course, everybody knows I married one of the cowboy greats, Tex Ritter.

EDITH FELLOWS

We shot RIDER OF DEATH VALLEY way out on location in Calabassas. It was *hot*. Tom Mix left no impression. I loved Tony—Mr. Mix put me up on top of Tony and rode me around. That was a thrill! Lois Wilson was the leading lady and she was the one who impressed me.

• • •

(regarding her movie, LAW OF THE LAWLESS, with Jack Hoxie) I must have had amnesia. After watching it, I don't recall a thing. I don't remember Majestic Studios. I do remember the name Jack Hoxie but not that I was in a picture with him. Actually, we had no scenes together. He was a bad actor, a little overweight. This movie wasn't released—it escaped!

EVELYN FINLEY

"Crash" Corrigan once told me if he were in charge of the films he would never use me. At first I was hurt. Then I asked him why. He smiled and said, "Because you're a better rider than any of the cowboys. You make us all look bad."

• • •

Tom Keene was a very nice and quiet man. I really didn't get to know him that well because he was somewhat of a loner. He wasn't temperamental or anything; he just didn't talk much to me or anyone else. He had a nice voice, was a good worker, and he was a very capable actor.

CAROL FORMAN

Serials were bread-and-butter films. You did them to eat, but you didn't go around bragging about them.

• • •

I had been in love with Tim Holt before I came to Holly-wood. I thought he was just the prettiest, cutest thing that could ever be. So while I was at the studio I was called to the producer's office one afternoon to talk about a part in a picture, and I walked in and looked right into the face of Tim Holt. And what kept my legs under me I'll never know, for I went weak all over—naturally, being around Tim, who I already idolized, caused me to fall in love with him, and as time went along he fell in love with me. For two-and-a-half years we were an item. Everybody thought we would get married, and we did make such plans but they never materialized.

ANN GWYNNE

I always enjoyed the westerns and I have many pleasant memories of them. Johnny Mack Brown was—truly—a Southern gentleman.

• • •

Bob Baker, who was a star at Universal before I got there, was doing secondary roles with Johnny Mack. When I did the Abbott and Costello western/comedy, RIDE 'EM COW-BOY, he only had a bit! I don't know why, but it was certainly a shame.

• • •

About KING OF THE BULLWHIP with Lash LaRue, I did it for the money. Most of it was stock footage. There were quite a few old timers in it—good people like Jack Holt, Michael Whalen, Dennis Moore, but it wasn't much of a picture, far below the quality I had experienced earlier.

LOIS HALL

Same thing everyone else said about him (Johnny Mack

Brown)—a true gentleman. And a little distant. He went back to his dressing room between things. But a pleasant person.

• • •

I always thought he (Whip Wilson) was a little arrogant. It might have been just me, but he seemed to have that thing about him a little bit, more than other people. Because western people, for the most part, are just great.

• • •

He (Charles Starrett) was, kind of like Johnny Mack, very gentlemanly when I was around, but a little aloof. Probably because he'd had such a succession of leading ladies and the shoots were so fast. Of the Charlie Starrett films, the thing I remember most is Fred Sears, the director, and his sweetness. A dear, dear man. Just a darling. A pure gentleman. I remember, too, the combination of Al Wyatt and Jocko Mahoney and the other stuntmen. I have always been fascinated with stuntmen.

RUTH HALL

I got along with Ken (Maynard), despite the fact that he was a rambunctious personality and got drunk a lot. I have been a Christian Scientist all my life. So I never went to work in the mornings before doing a great deal of praying. I know a lot of publicity came out that Ken was in love with me, but that was not true.

IRENE HERVEY

I was horseback riding and apparently touched the horse in the wrong place because he darted off at a fast pace with me hanging on like mad! Luckily, George (O'Brien) was also on horseback. He chased after me and rescued me! Just like in the movies!

WANDA HENDRIX
(actress and a wife of Audie Murphy)

Audie despised his father; he told me every time he shot one of the enemy during the war he pretended he was killing his father. Audie (because of the war) had the most terrible nightmares. He even slept with a loaded gun under his pillow.

JENNIFER HOLT

Tex Ritter was a precious individual. He was shy, courtly, and sweet—a real talent and one of God's gentlemen.

• • •

(When asked why her brother never had her in one of his films) Tim never asked! I don't know why he never asked. I could have certainly used the work—and the money.

KAY HUGHES

They asked me if I could ride a horse. Of course, I said I could. When you're young you feel like you can do anything. And I could ride a little; I'd been to a stable once or twice. They dressed me up in this beautiful, leather, divided skirt and put me on a horse ahead of a bunch of cowboys, and told us to ride fast into the scene. A small ditch had been dug to show us where to stop and stay within the camera frame. When my horse got to the spot, it stopped and I didn't. I went right over the animal's head and landed hard. I hurt my back and arm, so they put me in the studio bus and took me back to Republic. I didn't finish that picture, but I learned an extremely valuable lesson—always request a double.

• • •

Gene (Autry) was driven to location sites in a limousine, and I used to go with him. During these trips, he often used to sing to me in the car.

MARY BETH HUGHES

I started out with MGM and appeared in two films with Lana Turner. I got a glimpse of myself in the first picture, but in the second I missed myself altogether. At the preview I had dropped something and stooped to pick it up. In that instant occurred my brief appearance on the screen.

• • •

I enjoyed the westerns. I always thought my roles were a little different and more challenging than those of most western ladies.

• • •

(after three divorces and being single for some 20 years) I became stupid and married three alcoholics in a row and divorced them as fast as I could. Now I'm single again and intend to stay that way unless a millionaire comes along, which I seriously doubt will happen to me.

MARSHA HUNT

I saw Tom (Keene) just before he died at the Motion Picture County Hospital. He had really wasted away to skin and bones, eaten up with cancer. He died only two or three weeks later. I hesitated about it, but decided to go on and bring some old stills from DESERT GOLD to show him in the hospital. Fortunately, it worked out all right. He called the nurses to come and see what he looked like when he was young and healthy and, of course, he was so good-looking.

LOIS JANUARY

Bob Baker and Bob Steele were great guys who just made it fun to be in a western with. (Rating the riders) Fred Scott, Bob Baker, Bob Steele and Tim McCoy—solid 10. Johnny Mack Brown, an 8-1/2.

• • •

I loved making westerns. I am a Texas gal and being outside riding horses, getting to know the cowboys, playing exciting scenes with handsome men—well, for an 18 year old girl, I had it all!

• • •

We had more fun making those westerns. I used to take a lot of teasing from the boys in the company because of the way I go on a horse. I had been a dancer and knew how to lift my leg without bending it. Unconsciously, every time I'd mount up, my leg would go straight up in the air and everyone would laugh.

ANNE JEFFREYS

Working with Bill Elliott was wonderful. I even got to sing a

MARY ELLEN KAY

I enjoyed my work in westerns. I worked with many of the great cowboys like Rex Allen, Charles Starrett, Allan Lane and Bill Elliott. They were all nice to me. Maybe it was because I was so little.

ELYSE KNOX

Roy (Rogers) is a terrific person! I remember he'd just come back from a publicity tour and his station wagon was covered with initials his fans carved onto the car. I always liked his singing a lot. I only regret I didn't do more than one picture with him.

NAN LESLIE

I loved it (making westerns). I was a horseback rider, and I loved the locations and being out-of-doors. In between scenes I could ride the horses, and the wranglers, and the stuntmen on the set were so great to work with. I truly believe they selected me a lot of times because I could ride.

• • •

(regarding her romance with Tim Holt) We had a lot of plans for a while; he was in the midst of a divorce at the time. I was just enchanted by him because he was the perfect cowboy. He knew what he was doing on a horse, and he was certainly always the gentleman off the horse, and he was very protective of me and, oddly enough, a little shy at times. He was a special guy.

KAY LINAKER

The only B-western I ever made was BLACK ACES. It was a good part as parts in westerns went. I did more than watch the hero ride off into the sunset. I actually crossed the Kern River on the old swing bridge. No one told me the weight of my body forced the boards to rise to meet my feet with each step. With the wind swinging the bridge from side to side, looking down at the Kern River forty feet below boiling over the rocks, holding my hat on my head (I had just taken it from one of the "heavies" and it had no chin strap) and hanging onto the handhold cable—it was the longest block and a half I ever walked. Buck Jones was furious with the director, Les Selander. If I'm not mistaken, Les's credit does not appear on the crawl. The stunt girl, Aline Goodwin, was furious. She was done out of a fat fee and felt it absolutely cruel to put me through such trauma. I heartily agreed—but the scene is effective. Buck Jones was one of God's good gentlemen and an honor to the motion picture business.

LUCILLE LUND

When Reb (Russell) was signed for the movies, they thought it would be great to have another alumni of Northwestern play opposite him, and that's how I was cast in those two pictures. They were terrible movies—the worst of the worst. Reb was an nice man—he must have been divorced by this time, as we dated a few times. He was a perfect gentleman, who always wore expensive cowboy boots, even on our dates! Reb was not an actor—he couldn't act his way out of a paper bag, but he was so congenial, friendly, nice. Portly, but a nice-looking man.

BETH MARION

I've seen stills and lobby cards of FRONTIER SCOUT featuring George Houston and myself, but for the life of me I don't remember George Houston.

• • •

He (Tom Tyler) was a very handsome fellow. Very happily married. He also drove me back to town one time; we had a nice long visit. I was really shocked to hear he'd died early in life. He had surgery for, I believe, an ulcer and they cut the Vagus nerve. From then on, his health went right down. I always thought, more than over pronouncing his words, he maybe had a little accent and was trying to overcome that.

VIRGINIA MAYO

I had a love scene with Burt Lancaster, and he was supposed to be angry at me. He grabbed me and kissed me so violently I thought I'd lost my teeth. My arms turned black and blue. I surely didn't want to kiss him again.

• • •

I made a movie with Randolph Scott called WESTBOUND, but I hardly got to know the man because my part was so tiny. I was supposed to be the star, but the director (Budd Boetticher) gave the best part to his girl friend (Karen Steele). I didn't like that at all!

• • •

I don't know why you people want to come down here (Raleigh Film Festival) and watch these old worn out westerns.

FAY McKENZIE

Gene (Autry) was just a gracious, wonderful man to work with! He was so supportive. You know, I had worked in pictures since I was a small child, but I was just starting to do grown-up parts at the time—and Gene was the biggest star in the world. I mean, *nobody* was a bigger star. He was topping the list throughout the world. So I was in awe—totally in awe just to be in the room where he was. It was a marvelous opportunity for me—and DOWN MEXICO WAY was a little higher budget. Being the first one I did with Gene, it was exciting. He was really wonderful to work with.

• • •

Smiley (Burnette) was just a love! I mean, he was the type person you just wanted to hug; he was so sweet. He was just as nice as he appears on screen. When we were on location, he'd pick up his guitar and start singing, and pretty soon we'd all be singing together. He was just so special, and so funny—and adorable.

CONSTANCE MOORE

Bob Baker couldn't act, and neither could I at the time. At least I didn't think I could. I did sing, and had sung on the radio in Dallas, but they didn't use my voice in the "oaters." Bob sang, and he was very good. I haven't seen those films since I made them, and I have a feeling they don't hold up too well.

PAULINE MOORE

My memories of Sammy (Sammy Baugh in the serial KING OF THE TEXAS RANGERS) is that of a gentleman and so very easy to work with. I marveled at how well he handled his body, seemingly effortless at whatever he was doing.

PEGGY MORAN

I went to an interview for Gene Autry's RHYTHM OF THE SADDLE. The agent told me, "Whatever they ask you, tell them yes—you can do it." Naturally they asked if I could ride and I told them "yes," although I really couldn't. So, I practiced for about a week. When we started the picture, I could hardly sit down. My whole fanny was sore and blistered! I have home movies showing later I did learn to ride properly. Now I can gallop and not let my fanny leave the saddle!

NELL O'DAY

I did like making westerns. I was quite a good rider before I made films because I had done a great deal of riding as a child. In the movies, I rode a great little horse named Shorty.

• • •

I made only one film with Bob Steele although I had known him years before when we used to double-date (with other people). He made westerns during most of his career, but when he played one of the leading roles in John Steinbeck's novel, OF MICE AND MEN, he proved what a fine and subtle actor he was. He had a sort of wonderful 19th century face. All the leading men I played with were fine horsemen, but I think Bob Steele had more finesse and style in his riding than anyone I have seen.

CECILIA PARKER

I made four pictures with Ken Maynard and I finally laid it right out for him. I said, "You pay my salary, but if you can't behave yourself and curb your language, you'll have to get another actress." He shaped up after that—at least, I never had any more trouble with him.

SHIRLEY PATTERSON

(On her first picture) I was supposed to ride up this bank, from the water's edge straight to this little house with a hitching post in front. They told me to mount the horse and I started climbing up on the wrong side of the saddle. The wrangler said, "Don't you know how to ride?" I said, "No, but don't tell anyone." So he got my foot in the stirrup and said, "Hang onto the reins and I'll tie them around the saddle horn." We heard the director yell, "Roll 'em," and the wrangler hit the horse so hard I shot up the bank, right past the hitching post, going through the trees. The side of my face got cut up from the pine needles. I put my head down on the saddle horn because the horse was trying to knock me off. After that, they had a stunt girl do my riding scenes.

• • •

I enjoyed working with Eddie Dean. He was always a perfect gentleman, and he had that beautiful voice.

• • •

Bill Elliott taught me how to ride; he really helped me out— Charles Starrett and I toured service camps here in the United States. We had a cute little western skit—I was dressed in a dance hall girl outfit with flowers in my hair.

JEAN PORTER

I got to ride Trigger (in SAN FERNANDO VALLEY)—and that was the highlight of the movie for me. That horse was human! He was truly a very smart animal. I had the second lead to Dale Evans. She was, and still is, one of the sweetest people, and Roy Rogers is one of the nicest guys you could possibly meet.

DOROTHY REVIER

I never saw Buck Jones or Jack Holt fool around with women. Both were kind, friendly, communicative, but impersonal—which, in my estimation, was truly commendable.

ELAINE RILEY

Working in westerns was just pure fun; I loved it! When I was growing up in New York, I learned to ride horses in Central Park so doing westerns was no problem for me.

• • •

When I first met him (Richard "Chito" Martin), I thought he was the most handsome man I ever saw; we've been married thirty-five years, and I still think he's the most handsome man I ever saw.

CLAIRE ROCHELLE

I recall in one of our films, my horse was supposedly running away with me. Bob (Steele) rode up alongside of me and by hooking his leg around mine brought me off my horse. We did many things like that —it was quite dangerous I suppose.

• • •

Bob Steele was a delightful person to work with. After several films it was like being family. We even made up our dialogue in a few scenes.

ANN RUTHERFORD

Making westerns was like being a child again. We played pretend all day. What a wonderful way to earn a living— dressing up in costumes and riding horses.

• • •

He (Fred "Snowflake" Toones) was wonderful; he was adorable. Everyone loved Snowflake and he was such a good actor with a wonderful sense of timing, which was some achievement considering we barely had time to rehearse—Snowflake was a pro; he was a darling man.

SHELIA RYAN

Allan Lane and I were married all of three months! We couldn't agree on anything. We just could not get along.

(author's note: Miss Ryan was later married to Pat Buttram.)

MARION SHILLING

In my first film with Buck Jones, I was trying to ride a horse, and I didn't know how. The horse was soon prancing around and not doing anything I wanted it to. Suddenly I heard someone laugh. I turned around and it was Buck. He smiled and said, "I do believe that's the best example I've seen of a horse riding a girl."

• • •

Buck Jones was such a wonderful person, and he took an interest in people. Even today, all these years after his death, when something gets me down, all I have to do is think of Buck and something he did, and immediately I feel better.

• • •

He (Tim McCoy) and I dated for awhile. He always so quiet, never made a pass. My mother liked him because he had "polish." Then suddenly, out of the blue, without any kind of build up, he said, "Marion, how about you and I going to Palm Springs for the weekend, and I'll teach you about life." Well, if you had known my mother I wouldn't have to add—I never made it to Palm Springs with Tim McCoy.

LOUISE STANLEY

It was Bob Steele who taught me how to do a "pony express" (whereby a rider mounts a horse while in motion). They have to grab the saddle horn with both hands and swing themselves aboard.

• • •

Johnny Mack Brown was a handsome Southern gentleman, but he was certainly no horseman.

ELEANOR STEWART

Jack (Luden) rode a horse like he and the horse were one. It was beautiful to watch. He was very nice. He wanted me to marry him. He and his mother were buying a house in Hollywood. He wanted me to come and meet his mother. I really wasn't interested in him, maybe I was just curious. He went to a military school. He had a good education. His uncle was the owner of Luden Coughdrops. In those days that was the only cough drop people used. It was a very wealthy company. For some reason, Jack never went into that. His mother was a very domineering woman—the most domineering person I've ever met. I just knew anything between Jack and I wouldn't work out.

• • •

Making westerns was a wonderful experience. Of course, there were times we had to get up at 4:30 in the morning, times we shot when it was over 100 degrees and sometimes when you had to crack ice off puddles. In one picture at Lone Pine it snowed during the night so they had to write that into the script.

• • •

The only problem I ever had with a horse was with Topper. Whenever they tried to take still pictures, Topper was terrible. He'd come up and nibble your shoulder. It was an honor to be in several Hopalong Cassidy pictures, including some of the last ones Bill (Boyd) made for Pop—I mean Harry—Sherman. Being a leading lady in one of Sherman's westerns means a lot—because you can be human—he lets you dress smartly, and, even against an 1880 setting, you have character. You get to shoot at the villain, intelligently help the hero! Something about working out of doors relaxes people. Cowboys are wonderful, kind, generous fellows. None of us in westerns felt tense or nervous.

PEGGY STEWART

Bill Elliott was a good man and a hard worker. He was well liked, very serious, and had a dry sense of humor. He liked kids but really did not know how to deal with them. He would shake hands with a kid and greet the youngster formally like he was an adult. That was just Bill's way.

• • •

I liked working with Lash LaRue. I thought he was a good

actor and underrated. I thought he could have gone further if he had gotten the chance. Lash would make a fine character actor.

• • •

Sunset Carson was really "green" when he started his series. Tom London and I spent a lot of hours teaching Sunset how to deliver his lines. I love Sunset; he's just like a brother.

• • •

Allan Lane was absolutely the dullest man I ever met. He had no sense of humor. You could not joke with Allan. He was always worrying about his appearance. He would try on several pair of jeans to get the ones that suited him. He was always looking for an outfit that made him look thinner in the rump. I used to call him "Bubble-Butt."

• • •

Jock Mahoney and Bill Elliott could both ride with a glass of water on their heads and never spill a drop. Of course, Sunset was a great rider too.

• • •

When we were making the B-westerns, I didn't even know who was watching them. I had no idea they would have a following after all these years.

• • •

I loved my work in the westerns—it was like being paid to play. You were young; the cowboy heroes were great guys—and you got to ride a horse every day.

LINDA STIRLING

The truth,is I had no skill whatsoever with horses and more than once the crew would find me sprawled in the dust or crumpled in the bushes somewhere after the horse ran away.

• • •

I did enjoy making the westerns and the serials. My favorite western was SANTA FE SADDLEMATES with Sunset Carson. Everyone knows me from the serial, THE TIGER WOMAN. They'll probably etch "The Tiger Woman" on my tombstone.

GALE STORM

(regarding movies with Roy Rogers) I remember concentrating very hard to get my lines right so those takes on horseback didn't have to be reshot any more than necessary. In some of the long shots I had doubles, but usually I had to grit my teeth and at least gallop out of, or into, the camera range. Somehow I got by.

• • •

I made a movie with Rod Cameron called STAMPEDE. Rod was a wonderful fellow, and he and his wife were friends of ours for a while. We noticed that his wife's mother was always with them. One day Rod left his wife to marry his mother-in-law.

JUNE STORY

I could ride a horse and I loved the outdoors. When they asked if I would like to make a series of westerns with Gene Autry—I jumped at the chance.

• • •

I just loved Smiley Burnette. He was a wonderful and caring man. After a long day of filming in the heat and dust, Smiley would get a pan of cool water and bathe and massage my feet. It was wonderfully refreshing. Smiley loved kids. He and his wife adopted six beautiful children.

• • •

I had spent quite a bit of time with Will Rogers, and I thought Gene Autry had a lot of Will's philosophy.

HELEN TALBOT

My last name was Darling. The studio decided that it wasn't appropriate and changed it. I didn't understand that. After all, they let Twinkle Watts use her real name.

RUTH TERRY

Unfortunately, I viewed a couple of western films that I was in. I wasn't impressed.

VIRGINIA VALE

I am amazed that there are so many fans of B-westerns! They are all so kind, appreciative and seem to care. Let me tell you, that appreciation and affection is returned full-fold. When I am at a film festival I just can't stay in my room when I am entitled to time off; I feel the fans should get my full attention. I hope we can get more younger people interested in the old B-westerns; we don't want the films and players to "ride off into the sunset."

• • •

I never saw George O'Brien use a double. After all he was a superb athlete and very strong. He could pick me up like I was a feather. Even though he was very masculine, strong and a star, he was very kind, soft-spoken and a very gentle gentleman.

• • •

If Joan Crawford were here (Roy Rogers Festival) I would be thrilled to shake her hand. If Clark Gable were here I would be thrilled to shake his hand—but tonight I was both thrilled and honored to meet and shake the hand of the gentleman, Roy Rogers.

JUNE VINCENT

Kirby (Grant) was a nice fellow, with a good singing voice that we seldom got to hear. In most of my westerns, in fact most of the movies I did at Columbia, I was the meanie, the bitch. Like COLORADO SUNDOWN (at Republic) with Rex Allen and even the musical, ARKANSAS SWING with the Hoosier Hot Shots, a terrific quartet who were also in SONG OF IDAHO. Off screen, I was friends with people I was nasty to in the pictures.

TWINKLE WATTS

Allan Lane treated me okay. He was friendly enough. He just wasn't the kind of man who would go around bouncing a little girl on his knee or anything. Later on when I would see him he would smile and say, "Hi Twinkle."

LOIS WILSON

I had never met Mr. Mix until the day we started shooting (RIDER OF DEATH VALLEY). During the following week or two, I did not like him. I don't know why. Then we went on location and I became acquainted with an entirely different man.

• • •

He (Tom Mix) complimented me on my riding ability and we started talking horses. I love them and was rather proud of my ability to ride. I found Tom a fascinating storyteller and our friendship grew from then on.

MARIE WINDSOR

William Elliott had a high academic and rather "socially best school" background. He couldn't hide that quality whatever his western garb might be. I always thought Bill as "the" western gentleman cowboy. Bill's personality was about the same, on camera or off, with his voice and mannerism.

• • •

HELLFIRE, should have been a "hot" western that would have changed my whole career. Studio owner, Herbert Yates, promised to spend a lot of money to sell the film. Mr. Yates suddenly got involved in trying to get the communist out of the industry. He made a little film called THE RED MENACE, which he spent a great amount of money to sell and did nothing for HELLFIRE.

GLORIA WINTERS

I still see Roy and Dale several times a year. They are just great, one of the highlights for anyone to work with. Roy is a great human being.

• • •

There was a scene where I was talking to Gene (Autry)— he sings a song. When he found out I could sing, he called the scriptwriters. They came to the set and handed me handwritten music to the tune of "Swing Low Sweet Chariot." I sang a warning as I walked down the ghost town street. I gave the handwritten sheet music, along with the script, to the Autry museum.

JOAN WOODBURY

Tim McCoy was a delight, a distinguished gentleman and a sensational rider, even in his older years.

Section V

PRODUCERS AND DIRECTORS

Ideally, the producer was a combination shrewd business-man, tough taskmaster and prudent cost accountant. In the case of B-westerns, the producers were more interested in making a fast buck than they were in art or creativity.

Since the films were so popular with the juvenile audience and since they could be made quickly, inexpensively and with minimum financial risk, the goal of the producer was to make a lot of pictures, get them in the theaters, reap some fast bucks, and then start the cycle all over again.

The director's life was a trying one. They worked long hours, usually in the heat and dust, often with inexperienced or inferior actors and with constant pressure from the producer "to get it in the can." Perhaps director Spencer Gordon Bennet described it best: "Working with low budgets, short schedules and harried producers the film director was really caught in the middle! He had to know how to 'cut his picture in the camera,' for example, to conserve film. He had to use inexperienced, yet capable, players in order to cut down the number of takes, too." Despite many obstacles facing the directors, they sometimes turned out little gems that could hold their own against larger production pictures.

EARL BELLAMY

He was one character. When he was in school he went by Holly Bane—but his name was Mike Ragan. If I got on a show he would call me right away and say, "I'm ready. I'm available." He was funny that way. 'Course I would hire him 'cause I liked him so darn much. If company was down, he'd do something just for kicks to spark things up. When he would get shot—supposed to die in the scene—everybody would gather 'round to watch because Holly would take five minutes before he was dead. We'd get a kick out of that.

• • •

I'd get up by the camera to watch him (Dub "Cannonball" Taylor) because he was so funny and I'd get to laughing so hard I'd have to stuff my handkerchief in my mouth so nobody would hear me laugh.

SPENCER GORDON BENNET

Bill Elliott admired Buck Jones and tried to fashion his screen work after him. This was true when he started at Columbia and still true when he joined Republic.

• • •

Bob Allen was a pleasure to work with; he was a actor who could deliver his lines with feeling and emotion.

• • •

(regarding Republic studio czar, Herbert Yates' extravagant spending of stockholders' money in an attempt to make his girlfriend, Vera Ralston, a major star) I didn't know Herbert Yates too well. Of course, one just couldn't work at the studio and not hear gossip, including comments about how one stage was simply given over to an ice skating rink which, when not used for Vera Ralstons films, was a private skating rink for Herbert Yates and Vera Ralston. In fact, a large battle by Republic stockholders was occasioned by Yates' interesting concessions to Miss Ralston, as I recall. Her films just didn't make any money and the minority stockholders at Republic finally raised hell. After all, Vera Ralston was a large woman, who didn't look graceful on ice skates. A Czechoslovakian skating champion she may have been, but she wasn't any screen competition for Sonya Henie.

BUDD BOETTICHER

Everybody knows Gilbert Roland gave the performance of his life in BULLFIGHTER AND THE LADY—but as far as my personal affection for him, I probably disliked him more than any other actor I've known. He was arrogant—impossible. He faked a lot of people—he called everybody "amigo" because he never knew their name.

THOMAS CARR

(regarding the six westerns for Lippert studio with Jimmy Ellison and Russell Hayden) I shot them in 29 days. We worked ourselves to death, but that's where my serial training came into play, because I laid all six pictures out like a serial. They were completely different stories but the same crew, and the same actors, except for a few exceptions, were in all the pictures. The same guy would be a sheriff in one, a dirty bank robber in another, and a doctor in the third. With all different parts, everyone had to be kept straight what part they were playing at any particular time. Some days I shot scenes from all six pictures. I got these six scripts and I had to put them together and shoot them on the same sets and change the furniture and props around so on the same day we could use a set for one picture in the morning and another after lunch, with the same actor in different roles.

• • •

(Robert) Horton was a little tough to work with. I was an actor for too long; I wouldn't put up with him. He thought he was the prima donna, the king of the hill. He wasn't going to pull any of that with me because I'd worked with Gary Cooper, with Claude Rains, and they listen to you, they do what you want, and then you come up with a guy like Horton who couldn't act his way out of a paper bag!

• • •

He (Jock Mahoney) was one of the greatest athletes I've ever met. He had tremendous power in his legs. The way he could jump! He moved like a cat. Oh, I thought a lot of him.

OLIVER DRAKE

Bob Livingston was a smart actor. He did not like westerns but he did them hoping something better would come along. He would get into a sequence with Corrigan—Ray didn't know any better, bless his heart—and the first thing you knew Bob would have him turned around so that the camera saw only Livingston's face....

• • •

I worked with Dave O'Brien and Jim Newill on the Texas Rangers series. It was during World War II, and the boys thought they were going to be drafted. Well, for some reason, if you were a farmer or a rancher, you were exempted from service. The boys bought a goat ranch! It nearly worked them to death taking care of those stinking goats. Every day they came on the set smelling awful. When the boys were called in for their physicals, they were both classified 4-F. They immediately sold the ranch to Jack Ingram, and he made a movie location out of it.

• • •

Guy Wilkerson was the comic in the Texas Rangers series. He was a pretty good comedian. He was tall and as skinny as a rail. I thought he was funnier than he was given credit for. He was good to work with and a pleasant fellow. Off camera, he was quiet and not funny at all. He worked in many other films. Every once in a while I'd be watching a big production picture and old Guy would show up in some small role.

• • •

Jack Hoxie was a very nice man with whom to work. Between takes, he and his wife would always sit in the car and go over the script. I thought this was a little unusual until one day I discovered why. One of the trade papers had given Jack's latest film a favorable review. I thought he would enjoy seeing it and I gave it to him when he came to my office. He stood there studying it for a long time before I noticed that he had the paper upside down. That's when he confided to me he could not read or write except for signing his name. Still, we seldom had trouble with dialogue, and I don't think many people ever learned of Jack's limitations.

JOHN ENGLISH

(regarding the making of low budget pictures) Above all else, you must remember that we produced pictures which were just grist for the producer's money mill. The profit on a feature or western which cost fifteen thousand or twenty thousand, might be only a couple or three thousand dollars. If you consider that, you'll understand why most independent producers pinched pennies, used standardized plots and streamlined production methods. It was dollars and cents, that's all. Whether a director was turning out serials, westerns, or features, the independent director was always accountable to the financial department more so than was the director at MGM, Paramount, or any other of the major firms.

EDWARD FINNEY

As to Tex Ritter's place in western films, I think he brought an authenticity to his characterizations, and a brand of singing that typified the cowboy—unlike any other star— and his interpretation was more real than any other.

• • •

Tex Ritter would not let people walk over him and stood up for what he thought was right and just. There were a few instances of this when the occasion arose. Tex was a very agreeable personality and was well liked. I personally found him to be a very happy person. I don't recall ever having a disagreeable moment with him.

HARRY FRASER

Hoot Gibson led a stormy life, yet all told, it was a wonderful life. He was one of the most generous cowpokes ever to ride the silver screen. He was always giving gifts—some of them very costly—to his countless friends and pals.

• • •

Among the newcomers was Bob Steele, a fresh young wholesome-looking American boy of the West—a new kind of cowboy. The audience took Steele to their hearts and kept him there.

• • •

Bill Cody's problem was he could not memorize lines, no

matter how hard he tried. As a result, it took eight or ten takes to get a sequence on film. That meant the budget, always rock bottom in those days, was being shot to pieces. When Bradbury (director Robert N.) finally had the first picture in the can, he vowed no more Cody films. I needed a job, and I got one, directing our western hero of no memory, Bill Cody. Well, I took care of that handicap in a hurry. I wrote a scene where Cody said, "I'm Silent Saunders." From then on, all our hero Cody had to say was "Yes," and "No," and sometimes "Maybe."

LAMBERT HILLYER

Tom Mix carried a complete stock company of cowboys from cooks to wranglers, and they all doubled him at times. However, this fact was considered top secret and not one of them would have admitted the fact to a stranger. Mix had guts to spare. Sometimes if he didn't like the way the stunt looked, he'd get sore and do it himself. Better not try to stop him, either. Mix was himself a good man with a rifle, rope and six-gun. Very fast on the draw and as a stagecoach driver, one of the best.

NAT LEVINE

I received a dozen letters from Autry in 1933 asking for an opportunity to work for me in anything I would suggest in pictures. Autry's name value was limited, too—a radio station in Chicago, practically an unknown with questionable ability. While he was good-looking, it seemed to me he lacked the commodity necessary to become a western star: Virility. I wasn't impressed and tried to give him a nice brush-off, telling him I would think about it. For a period of six months he wrote to me continually, conveying that he would do anything for the opportunity. I don't believe he ever acknowledged my contribution to his career, nor did I ever receive thanks.

PAUL MALVERN

(Bob) Steele and (John) Wayne were great to work with. (Rex) Bell, too, but Bell was married to Clara Bow at the time, and he was just concerned about her health a lot. Rex made just one series for us, that was all. Of the three, the best actor and horseman was Bob Steele. Bob could do all kinds of fancy mounts, was excellent with horses. Wayne and Bell were good. Of course, in long shots. we doubled all three of them. But Bob could do all kinds of tricks, like leapfrog over the rump of the horse and into the saddle, things like that. He was very clever.

• • •

One of the great things about George "Gabby" Hayes was his ability to look at a script a couple of times and tell you every line in it, not just his words but everyone else's. He had a photographic mind. And the more I learned how good an actor he was, the bigger his parts got.

GEORGE SHERMAN

Don Barry and I were good friends. In fact, I was his best man when he married Peggy Stewart. To be honest, Don was a hothead. He was always arguing with people and getting into trouble. Many times I had to intervene to calm him down. I was shocked and saddened to hear Don took his own life. I had talked to him on the phone the day before he shot himself.

• • •

I worked on the Three Mesquiteers series with Bob Livingston and Ray Corrigan. They didn't like each other very much. Corrigan thought he was getting short changed in the series, and Livingston thought he should be in bigger productions. Well, Livingston moved up to bigger things and was replaced in the series by John Wayne. Corrigan regarded Wayne about the same as he had Livingston, but it didn't bother Wayne one bit.

SAM SHERMAN

(regarding people's fascination with B-westerns) For those who understand, no explanation is necessary; for those who don't understand, no explanation is possible.

R. G. SPRINGSTEEN

I always tried to make working on a movie a family affair. I liked all the cowboys I worked with. I did quite a few Red Ryder films with Bill Elliott and Allan Lane. Bill was a nice man and great to work with. Allan Lane was a little tough at times, but we learned to get along pretty well.

• • •

I made three pictures with Audie Murphy. Audie was a pretty headstrong guy. You know he was the most decorated soldier in World War II. He wasn't pleased with the way he was supposed to deliver some lines in one of our scripts and told me emphatically he was not going to do it. I tried to argue with him but he became more determined. Then, I thought to myself, here I am arguing with a man who killed 200 Germans—and all I've ever done is bump off an alley cat. I changed the script!

BILL WITNEY

Nobody could stand Rocky Lane. He thought he was much better than he was. He couldn't ride worth a damn. I hate to even talk about the man.

• • •

Slim Pickens was funny on and off the screen. He was a great guy and one of the best riders I ever worked with.

• • •

He (one of the singing cowboys) was on stage making a personal appearance with his horse. He made the horse count his age, rear up and bow to the audience. He adjusted the microphone and was about to speak as the horse walked off the stage behind him, lifted his tail and relieved himself. The cowboy, unaware of this, spoke into the microphone. He said, "Now that my pal has done his little bit to entertain you, I'll do mine." The cowboy never used that line again.

• • •

MGM let Bob Livingston go and kept Robert Taylor—and Livingston was a better actor.

• • •

I knew him very well (Fred Toones). We all called him Snowflake. He was a wonderful guy and everyone loved him. He was a shoeshine boy at the studio. We would call down when we needed something or some errands run and Snowflake was always ready to help us out. We would often create a part for him in our pictures. He would come up to me and say, "Mr. Bill, I need some lettuce, you know, some of that green stuff," (meaning money). I'd write in a part for him and pay him something like thirty-five dollars. Snowflake was a swell guy and a lot of fun to be around.

• • •

Roy Rogers was a great athlete who could ride, fight, dive and jump with the best of the stuntmen. Of all the western leads I've worked with, I'd give him a perfect ten in horsemanship.

Section VI
MISCELLANEOUS

WHAT'S THAT COWGIRL'S NAME?

Screen Name	Birth Name
Jane "Poni" Adams	Betty Jane Pierce
Vivian Austin	Vivian Coe
Joan Barclay	Geraine Greer
Madge Bellamy	Margaret Philpot
Pamela Blake	Adele Pearce
Adrian Booth/Lorna Gray	Virginia Pound
Reno Browne/Blair	Ruth Clarke
Phyllis Coates	Gypsie Ann Stell
Lois Collier	Madelyn Jones
Carolina Cotton	Helen Hagstrom
Gail Davis	Betty Jean Grayson
Penny Edwards	Millicent Edwards
Dale Evans	Frances Octavia Smith
Dorothy Fay	Dorothy Fay Southward
Jane Frazee	Mary Jane Freshe
Shirley Grey	Agnes Zetterstrand
Anne Gwynne	Marguerite Twice
Jennifer Holt	Elizabeth Holt
Anne Jeffreys	Anne Carmichael
Mary Lee	Mary Lee Wooters
Beth Marion	Beth Geottche
Virginia Mayo	Virginia Jones
Dorothy Revier	Doris Velegra
Marjorie Reynolds	Marjorie Goodspeed
Sheila Ryan	Katherine McLaughlin
Louise Stanley	Louise Keys
Peggy Stewart	Peggy O'Rourke
Linda Stirling	Louise Schultz
June Storey	June McTeer
Gale Storm	Josephine Cottle
Helen Talbot	Helen Darling
Ruth Terry	Ruth McMahon
Virginia Vale	Dorothy Howe
Jacqueline Wells/Julie Bishop	Jacqueline Brown

WHAT'S THAT COWBOY'S NAME?

Screen Name	Real Name
Bob Allen	Theodore Baehr
Bronco Billy Anderson	Max Aaronson
Slim Andrews	Lloyd Andrews
Bob Baker	Stanley Leland Weed
Roy Barcroft	Howard Ravenscroft
Buzz Barton	William Lamoreaux
Gregg Barton	Hal Barker
Don Barry	Don Barry DeAcosta
Rex Bell	George Beldon
Bruce Bennett	Herman Brix
Bobby Blake (Little Beaver)	Michael Gubitosi
Monte Blue	Montgomery Bluefeather
Lane Bradford	John Myrtland LeVarre Jr.
Buffalo Bill Jr.	Jay Wilsey
Rory Calhoun	Francis Timothy Durgin
Rod Cameron	Roderick Cox
Rocky Camron	Gene Alsace
Yakima Canutt	Enos Canutt
Sunset Carson	Michael Wayne Harrison
Lon Chaney Jr.	Creighton Chaney
Lane Chandler	Robert Oakes
Gary Cooper	Frank James Cooper
Ray "Crash" Corrigan	Ray Bernard
Buster Crabbe	Clarence Linden Crabbe
Bob Custer	Raymond Glenn
Dick Curtis	Richard Dye
Ken "Festus" Curtis	Curtis Gates
Rufe Davis	Rufus Davidson
Richard Dix	Ernest Brimmer
Kirk Douglas	Issur Danielovitch Demsky
Kenne Duncan	Kenneth Duncan MacLachlan
Bill Elliott	Gordon Nance
Jimmy Ellison	James Ellison Smith
Tex Fletcher	Jerry Bisceglia
Dick Foran	John Nicholas Foran
Hoot Gibson	Edmund Gibson
Kirby Grant	Kirby Grant Hoon
Russell Hayden	Pate Lucid
Pee Wee Holmes	Gilbert Holmes
Jack Holt	Charles John Holt Jr.
Tim Holt	Charles John Holt III
Will Hutchins	Marshall Hutchason

Si Jenks..Howard Jenkins
Buck Jones.. Charles Gebhard
Tom Keene..George Duryea
John "Dusty" King................................Miller McLeod Everson
Fuzzy Knight ....John Forrest Knight
Allan "Rocky" Lane .... Harry Albershart
Lash LaRue.. Alfred LaRue
Robert Livingston .... Robert Randall
Tom London ....Leonard Clapham
Cactus Mack .... Taylor McPeters
Guy Madison .... Robert Moseley
Jock Mahoney .... Jacques O'Mahoney
Lee Majors .... Harvey Lee Yeary
John Merton .... John Myrtland LeVarre Sr.
Art Mix .... George Kesterson
Dennis Moore ....Dennis Meadows
Bob Nolan .... Robert Nobles
Hugh O'Brian.. Hugh Krampke
Dave O'Brien.. David Barclay
Bud Osborne ....Lennie Osborne
Jack O'Shea... Jack Belaford
Slim Pickens....................................Louis Bert Lindley Jr.
Snub Pollard.. Harold Frazier
Jack Randall...Addison Randall
Tex Ritter.....................................Woodward Maurice Ritter
Roy Rogers .... Leonard Sly
Gilbert Roland ....Luis Alonso
Buddy Roosevelt .... Kent Sanderson
Gene Roth ....Gene Stutenroth
Reb Russell .... LaFayette Russell
Syd Saylor .... Leo Sailor
Jay Silverheels (Tonto) ....Harold J. Smith
Snowflake... Fred Toones
Bob Steele.. Robert Adrian Bradbury
Tom Steele .... Tom Skeoch
Hal Taliaferro/Wally Wales .... Floyd Alderson
Dub "Cannonball" Taylor .... Walter Taylor
Robert Taylor .... Spangler Arlington Brugh
Chief Thundercloud .... Victor Daniels
Tom Tyler .... Vincent Markowski
James Warren..James Wittlig
John Wayne .... Marion Michael Morrison
Wally West .... Theo Wynn
Whip Wilson .... Roland Charles Myers
Hank Worden .... Norton Worden

MOVIE HORSES

Many of the movie horses enjoyed a popularity almost equal to the movie cowboy. Since I am often asked the name of a B-western cowboy's horse, I have provided the following list as a handy reference guide.

Art Acord .... Raven
Bob Allen .... Pal
Rex Allen .... Koko
Slim Andrews .... Josephine (mule)
Gene Autry .... Champion
Bob Baker .... Apache
Smith Ballew .... Sheik
Jim Bannon .... Thunder
Don Barry .... Cyclone
Bobby "Little Beaver" Blake .... Papoose
William "Hoppy" Boyd .... Topper
Johnny Mack Brown .... Reno/Rebel
Reno Browne .... Major
Smiley Burnette .... Nelly/Ringeye
Rod Cameron .... Knight
Leo "Pancho" Carrillo .... Loco
Sunset Carson .... Silver/Cactus
Andy Clyde .... Johnny
Bill Cody .... Chico
Don Coleman .... Ghost
Buster Crabbe .... Falcon
Gail "Annie Oakley" Davis .... Target
Eddie Dean .... White Cloud/ Copper/Flash
William Desmond .... Chief/Beauty/Shamrock
Bill Elliott .... Sonny/Thunder
Dale Evans .... Buttermilk
Hoot Gibson .... Starlight/Mud/Goldie
Dick Foran .... Smoke or Smokey
Monte Hale .... Pardner
William S. Hart .... Fritz
Tim Holt .... Duke/Lightning
Jack Hoxie .... Scout
Buck Jones .... Silver
Tom Keene .... Rusty/Prince/Flash
Fuzzy Knight .... Old Brownie
Rocky Lane .... Feather/Thunder/Blackjack
Lash LaRue .... Black Diamond/Rush
Bob Livingston .... Starlight/Shamrock

Jack Luden .... Pal
Guy Madison .... Buckshot
Richard "Chito" Martin .... Taco
Ken Maynard .... Tarzan
Kermit Maynard .... Rocky
Tim McCoy .... Starlight/Midnight
Tom Mix .... Old Blue/Tony
Clayton Moore .... Silver
Pete Morrison .... Lightning
Nell O'Day .... Shorty
George O'Brien .... Mike
Dorothy Page .... Snowy
Jack Perrin .... Starlight
Slim Pickens .... John
Jack Randall .... Rusty
Duncan "Cisco" Renaldo .... Diablo
Tex Ritter .... White Flash
Roy Rogers .... Trigger
Reb Russell .... Rebel
Fred Scott .... White Dust
Randolph Scott .... Stardust
Jay "Tonto" Silverheels .... Scout
Charles Starrett .... Raider
Bob Steele .... Zane
James Stewart .... Pie
Peggy Stewart .... Smoky
Roy Stewart .... Ranger
Fred Thomson .... Silver King
Tom Tyler .... Ace/Baron
Jimmy Wakely .... Lucky/Sonny
Wally Wales .... Silver King
John Wayne .... Duke/Dollar
Whip Wilson .... Silver Bullet

TOP TEN MONEY-MAKING WESTERN STARS
by Bobby J. Copeland

In 1936 the *Motion Picture Herald* initiated a poll in an attempt to determine the Top Ten Money-Making Western Stars. In reality, the poll only measured the popularity of B-western stars as rated by the *theater operators*. While most B-western historians will probably agree that the top two or three stars in each year's poll do reflect the top money-makers, many will also agree that the rest of the rankings were purely guess work. This guess work may explain the following questionable rankings:

1. Smiley Burnette, while serving as a sidekick to Charles Starrett, was *twice* ranked above Starrett. Surely the fans did not go to the theaters to see Burnette over Starrett, who was then portraying the very popular Durango Kid.

2. In 1946, Fuzzy Knight who was appearing as Kirby Grant's sidekick. was ranked ninth and Grant was not even listed.

3. Four sidekicks made the poll: Smiley Burnette, Gabby Hayes, Andy Devine. and Fuzzy Knight. However, Fuzzy St John, who appeared as a sidekick to more western stars than any other actor, never made it.

4. Dale Evans, the only female to appear in the rankings, made the list four times, which was more than such stars as Allan "Rocky" Lane, Bob Steele, Buster Crabbe, Sunset Carson, and Eddie Dean (Lash LaRue, Monte Hale, Jimmy Wakely, and Whip Wilson were never even ranked).

5. From 1936 to 1945, Tex Ritter appeared on the list seven times - and with five different studios. However, if Ritter was such a money-maker why did he find difficulty in remaining at one studio for an extended period of time - and why did he not make a starring film after 1945? It should also be noted that Ritter was teamed for a while with Bill Elliott and then with Johnny Mack Brown. Although Ritter received equal billing with those stars, it must be obvious to those who have viewed the films that he was not equal. Ritter concluded

his starring career at lowly PRC, where he was not the star - or even part of a duo - but part of a trio called The Texas Rangers.

6. George Hayes, who appeared on the poll eleven times, did not make it in 1953. Yet, he returned to the number five spot in 1954, although he had made no films since 1950!

7. Allan Lane, who made some of the finest B-western films, is on almost every fan's list as a favorite cowboy star. However, he did not make the list until 1951.

8. Roy Rogers maintained his number one slot in 1952 and 1953, although Rogers made no films. Gene Autry, who remained at number two, made six films in each of those years. Rogers and Autry held their positions in 1954, when neither made a movie.

The poll continued until 1954. However, it probably should have ended in 1952, for the era of B-westerns was coming to an end due to the popularity of television. Because of the decline in the films, the 1953 and 1954 polls only ranked five stars. In 1954, the five stars made a total of three films.

Although the poll should not be considered as an official ranking of the Top Ten Money-Making Western Stars, it does provide a subject for interesting conversation and debate. Despite its short comings, it is better than no poll at all.

Note: The number in parenthesis indicates the previous year's ranking.

1936	1937
1. Buck Jones	1. Gene Autry (3)
2. George O'Brien	2. William Boyd (4)
3. Gene Autry	3. Buck Jones (1)
4. William Boyd	4. Dick Foran (6)
5. Ken Maynard	5. George O'Brien (2)
6. Dick Foran	6. Tex Ritter (0)
7. John Wayne	7. Three Mesquiteers (0)
8. Tim McCoy	8. Charles Starrett (0)
9. Hoot Gibson	9. Ken Maynard (5)
10. Buster Crabbe	10. Bob Steele (0)

1938

1. Gene Autry (1)
2. William Boyd (2)
3. Buck Jones (3)
4. George O'Brien (5)
5. Three Mesquiteers (7)
6. Charles Starrett (8)
7. Bob Steele (10)
8. Smith Ballew (0)
9. Tex Ritter (6)
10. Dick Foran (4)

1939

1. Gene Autry (1)
2. William Boyd (2)
3. Roy Rogers (0)
4. George O'Brien (4)
5. Charles Starrett (6)
6. Three Mesquiteers (5)
7. Tex Ritter (9)
8. Buck Jones (3)
9. John Wayne (0)
10. Bob Baker (0)

1940

1. Gene Autry (1)
2. William Boyd (2)
3. Roy Rogers (3)
4. George O'Brien (4)
5. Charles Starrett (5)
6. Johnny Mack Brown (0)
7. Tex Ritter (7)
8. Three Mesquiteers (6)
9. Smiley Burnette (0)
10. Bill Elliott (0)

1941

1. Gene Autry (1)
2. William Boyd (2)
3. Roy Rogers (3)
4. Charles Starrett (5)
5. Smiley Burnette (9)
6. Tim Holt (0)
7. Johnny Mack Brown (6)
8. Three Mesquiteers (8)
9. Bill Elliott (10)
10. Tex Ritter (7)

1942

1. Gene Autry (1)
2. Roy Rogers (3)
3. William Boyd (2)
4. Smiley Burnette (5)
5. Charles Starrett (4)
6. Johnny Mack Brown (7)
7. Bill Elliott (9)
8. Tim Holt (6)
9. Don Barry (0)
10. Three Mesquiteers (8)

1943

1. Roy Rogers (2)
2. William Boyd (3)
3. Smiley Burnette (4)
4. Gabby Hayes (0)
5. Johnny Mack Brown (6)
6. Tim Holt (8)
7. Three Mesquiteers (10)
8. Don Barry (9)
9. Bill Elliott (7)
10. Russell Hayden (0)

1944

1. Roy Rogers (1)
2. William Boyd (2)
3. Smiley Burnette (3)
4. Gabby Hayes (4)
5. Bill Elliott (9)
6. Johnny Mack Brown (6)
7. Don Barry (8)
8. Charles Starrett (0)
9. Russell Hayden (10)
10. Tex Ritter (0)

1945

1. Roy Rogers (1)
2. Gabby Hayes (2)
3. William Boyd (2)
4. Bill Elliott (5)
5. Smiley Burnette (3)
6. Johnny Mack Brown (6)
7. Charles Starrett (8)
8. Don Barry (7)
9. Tex Ritter (10)
10. Rod Cameron (0)

1946
1. Roy Rogers (1)
2. Bill Elliott (4)
3. Gene Autry (0)
4. Gabby Hayes (2)
5. Smiley Burnette (5)
6. Charles Starrett (7)
7. Johnny Mack Brown (6)
8. Sunset Carson (0)
9. Fuzzy Knight (0)
10. Eddie Dean (0)

1947
1. Roy Rogers (1)
2. Gene Autry (3)
3. William Boyd (0)
4. Bill Elliott (2)
5. Gabby Hayes (4)
6. Charles Starrett (6)
7. Smiley Burnette (5)
8. Johnny Mack Brown (7)
9. Dale Evans (0)
10. Eddie Dean (10)

1948
1. Roy Rogers (1)
2. Gene Autry (2)
3. Bill Elliott (4)
4. Gabby Hayes (5)
5. William Boyd (3)
6. Charles Starrett (6)
7. Tim Holt (0)
8. Johnny Mack Brown (7)
9. Smiley Burnette (7)
10. Andy Devine (0)

1949
1. Roy Rogers (1)
2. Gene Autry (2)
3. Gabby Hayes (4)
4. Tim Holt (7)
5. Bill Elliott (3)
6. Charles Starrett (6)
7. William Boyd (5)
8. Johnny Mack Brown (8)
9. Smiley Burnette (9)
10. Andy Devine

1950
1. Roy Rogers (1)
2. Gene Autry (2)
3. Gabby Hayes (3)
4. Bill Elliott (5)
5. William Boyd (7)
6. Tim Holt (4)
7. Charles Starrett (6)
8. Johnny Mack Brown (8)
9. Smiley Burnette (9)
10. Dale Evans (0)

1951
1. Roy Rogers (1)
2. Gene Autry (2)
3. Tim Holt (6)
4. Charles Starrett (7)
5. Rex Allen (0)
6. Bill Elliott (4)
7. Smiley Burnette (9)
8. Allan Lane (0)
9. Dale Evans (10)
10. Gabby Hayes (3)

1952
1. Roy Rogers (1)
2. Gene Autry (2)
3. Rex Allen (5)
4. Bill Elliott (6)
5. Tim Holt (3)
6. Gabby Hayes (10)
7. Smiley Burnette (7)
8. Charles Starrett (4)
9. Dale Evans (9)
10. William Boyd (0)

1953
1. Roy Rogers (1)
2. Gene Autry (2)
3. Rex Allen (3)
4. Bill Elliott (4)
5. Allan Lane (0)

1954
1. Roy Rogers (1)
2. Gene Autry (2)
3. Rex Allen (3)
4. Bill Elliott (4)
5. Gabby Hayes (0)

The following list includes everyone who ever appeared in the Top Ten Money Making Western Stars. The number in parenthesis indicates the number of years that the person made the list.

Gene Autry (16)	Dick Foran (3)
Roy Rogers (16)	Eddie Dean (2)
Bill Elliott (15)	Andy Devine (2)
William Boyd (14)	Russell Hayden (2)
Charles Starrett (14)	Allan Lane (2)
Smiley Burnette (13)	Ken Maynard (2)
Johnny Mack Brown (11)	Bob Steele (2)
Gabby Hayes (11)	John Wayne (2)
Tim Holt (8)	Bob Baker (l)
Three Mesquiteers (7)	Smith Ballew (1)
Tex Ritter (7)	Rod Cameron (l)
George O'Brien (5)	Sunset Carson (l)
Rex Allen (4)	Buster Crabbe (1)
Don Barry (4)	Hoot Gibson (l)
Dale Evans (4)	Fuzzy Knight (1)
Buck Jones (4)	Tim McCoy (l)

Author's footnotes:

(a) Gene Autry received ranking three times in the Top Ten *of all* Hollywood Money-Making Stars. In 1940 he was fourth, in 1941 he was sixth, and in 1942 he was seventh.
(b) Roy Rogers was ranked tenth on the same list in 1945.
(c) Autry was ranked number one on the Top Ten Money-Making Western Poll from 1937-1942, when he volunteered for the U.S. Army Air Corps.
(d) Roy Rogers took over the number one spot in 1943 and held it for the duration of the poll.
(e) Autry returned to film-making in 1946.
(f) In 1943, the cowboy stars from Republic Pictures captured six of ten places on the poll.
(g) Tim Holt made no western films in 1943,1944 and 1945, when he was serving in the armed forces.
(h) Charles Starrett, who made the list 14 times, had his streak broken in 1943 despite making six pictures that year. *Strangely enough* Russell Hayden, who had played a supporting role in the Starrett Films the previous year, placed tenth in 1943.

COWBOYS AT REST
Burial Locations of Western Stars
(C) indicates cremated

Name	Cemetery	City	State
Art Acord	Forest Lawn	Glendale	CA
Bronco Billy Anderson	Chapel of the Pines (C)	Los Angeles	CA
Roscoe Ates	Forest Lawn	Glendale	CA
Bob Baker	Clearcreek	Camp Verde	AZ
Smith Ballew	Laurel Land	Fort Worth	TX
Jim Bannon	(C)		
Buzz Barton	Eternal Valley	Newhall	CA
Rex Bell	Forest Lawn	Glendale	CA
Monte Blue	Forest Lawn	Glendale	CA
William Boyd	Forest Lawn	Glendale	CA
Johnny Mack Brown	Forest Lawn	Glendale	CA
Smiley Burnette	Forest Lawn	Hollywood Hills	CA
Leo Carrillo	Woodland	Santa Monica	CA
Andy Clyde	Forest Lawn	Glendale	CA
Chuck Connors	San Fernando	Santa Barbara	CA
Gary Cooper	Sacred Heart	Long Island	NY
Andy Devine	Pacific View	Newport Beach	CA
Hoot Gibson	Inglewood Park	Inglewood	CA
William S. Hart	Greenwood	Brooklyn	NY
Ray Corrigan	Inglewood Park	Inglewood	CA
Russell Hayden	Oakwood Park	Chatsworth	CA
Gabby Hayes	Forest Lawn	Glendale	CA
Tim Holt	Memory Lane	Harrah	OK
Bill Elliott	Palm Mortuary (C)	Las Vegas	NV
Buck Jones	(C)	Pacific Ocean	
Michael Landon	Hillside Memorial	Los Angeles	CA
Allan Lane	Inglewood Park	Inglewood	CA
Ken Maynard	Forest Lawn	Glendale	CA
Kermit Maynard	Valhalla Community (C)	Los Angeles	CA
Tim McCoy	Mt. Olivet (C)	Saginaw	MI
Tom Mix	Forest Lawn	Glendale	CA
Wayne Morris	Arlington	Arlington	VA
Audie Murphy	Arlington	Arlington	VA
Bob Nolan	(C)	(the desert)	
George O'Brien.	(C)	Pacific Ocean	
Dorothy Page	Allen Union	Northampton	PA
Snub Pollard	Forest Lawn	Hollywood Hills	CA
Jack Randall	Forest Lawn	Glendale	CA
Duncan Renaldo	Calvary	Santa Barbara	CA
Lynne Roberts	Forest Lawn	Hollywood Hills	CA
Randolph Scott	Elmwood	Charlotte	NC
Jay Silverheels	(C)	(Ashes returned to Canada)	
Bob Steele	Forest Lawn (C)	Hollywood Hills	CA
Chief Thundercloud	Forest Lawn	Glendale	CA
Tom Tyler	Mt. Olivet	Detroit	MI
John Wayne	Pacific View	Newport Beach	CA
Grant Withers	Forest Lawn	Glendale	CA

COWBOY CREEDS
The Lone Ranger Creed

I believe:

That to have a friend, a man must be one.

That all men are created equal and that everyone has within himself the power to make this a better world.

That God put the firewood there, but every man must gather and light it himself.

In being prepared physically, mentally and morally to fight when necessary, for that which is right.

That a man should make the most of what equipment he has.

That "This government, of the people, by the people, and for the people" shall live always.

That men should live by the rule of what is best for the greatest number.

That sooner or later, somewhere, somehow, we must settle with the world and make payment for what we have taken.

That all things change but truth, and that truth alone lives on forever.

In my Creator, my country, my fellow man.

Roy Rogers Riders Club Rules

1. Be neat and clean.
2. Be courteous and polite.
3. Always obey your parents.
4. Protect the weak and help them.
5. Be brave but never take chances.
6. Study hard and learn all you can.
7. Be kind to animals and care for them.
8. Eat all your food and never waste any.
9. Love God and go to Sunday School regularly.
10. Always respect our flag and our country.

Creed of the Buck Jones Rangers of America

AS A BUCK JONES RANGER:

I must be courteous and obedient to my elders.

I must study and learn.

I must be courageous, honest, industrious, truthful and unselfish.

I must be a pal to my playmates and big brother (or sister) to all boys and girls younger than myself.

I must keep my daily life bright and clean.

Gene Autry's Cowboy Commandments

1. He must not take unfair advantage of an enemy.
2. He must never go back on his word.
3. He must always tell the truth.
4. He must be gentle with children, elderly people and animals.
5. He must not possess racially or religiously intolerant ideas.
6. He must help people in distress.
7. He must be a good worker.
8. He must respect women, parents and his nation's laws.
9. He must neither drink nor smoke.
10. He must be a patriot.

Hopalong Cassidy Creed for American Boys and Girls

1. The highest honor a person can wear is honesty. Be truthful at all times.
2. Your parents are the best friends you have. Listen to them and obey their instructions.
3. If you want to be respected, you must respect others. Show good manners in every way.
4. Only through hard work and study can you succeed. Don't be lazy.
5. Your good deeds always come to light. So don't boast or be a show-off.
6. If you waste time or money today, you will regret it tomorrow. Practice thrift in all ways.
7. Many animals are good and loyal companions. Be friendly and kind to them.
8. A strong, healthy body is a precious gift. Be neat and clean.
9. Our country's laws are made for your protection. Observe them carefully.
10. Children in many foreign lands are less fortunate than you. Be glad and proud you are an American.

Roy Rogers Riders Club Prayer

Oh Lord, I reckon I'm not much just by myself. I fail to do a lot of things I ought to do. But Lord, when trails are steep and passes high, help me to ride it straight the whole way through. And when in the falling dusk I get the final call, I do not care how many flowers they send—above all else the happiest trail would be for You to say to me, "Let's ride, My friend."

Amen.

The Lone Ranger's Health and Safety Club Rules

As a Health and Safety Ranger,
I Promise to Obey my Solemn Pledge to
THE LONE RANGER.

I solemnly promise:
1. To take plenty of healthy outdoor exercise.
2. To brush my teeth in the morning and at night.
3. To eat nourishing food and well-balanced meals.
4. To eat all the food I am served.
5. To wash my hands before every meal.
6. Not to put my hands to my mouth after touching pets and other animals, without washing my hands.
7. To wear warm clothes in cold weather; to keep my feet dry in wet weather.
8. To prevent falls by not leaving bicycle, scooter, skates or toys lying around.
9. Not to play with matches and to protect my home from danger of fire.
10. Not to cross streets against traffic signals nor play in the street.
11. To encourage fair play among my friends, good habits and respect for other people's property.
12. To obey my parents or guardians and help my country in every way I can.

The Lone Ranger's Code of the West

The Lone Ranger is **Honest**—
Honesty is being truthful, sincere and straightforward.
The Lone Ranger is **Fair**—
Fairness is being open-minded and committed to the equitable treatment of all.
The Lone Ranger is **Caring**—
Caring is showing kindness, generosity and compassion toward others.
The Lone Ranger is **Respectful**—
Respect means not taking advantage of others as well as being polite and courteous.
The Lone Ranger is **Loyal**—
Loyalty means a faithfulness to commitments and obligations to family, friends, community and country but most importantly, to principle.
The Lone Ranger is **Tolerant**—
Tolerance is the ability to accept differences and not judge people harshly because they are different.
The Lone Ranger does his **Duty**—
Doing your duty means being responsible and accountable for your actions. It means earnest thought before action.
The Lone Ranger is **Morally Courageous**—
Moral courage is the inner strength to overcome obstacles or compelling forces to do what *should* be done, no matter the personal consequences.

The Smiley Burnette Fan Club Pledge

I promise to make every effort to see Smiley "Frog" Burnette in every picture he is in.
I promise always to let my friends know where and when they can see "Frog" in pictures.
I promise to show my loyalty to "Frog" by writing him once each month faithfully and will offer constructive and helpful suggestions regarding his pictures.
I promise to show my interest in our club by doing everything I can to get new members.
I promise to carry my membership card with me at all times and to obey the pledges guiding our fan club.

MOVIE COWBOYS' THEME SONGS

Rough Riders Theme Song

The Rough Riders ride beware;
The Rough Riders ride take care.
They're the finest bunch in the land...
Chasing every rustler and guerrilla band.
The Rough Riders watch the trail;
The Rough Riders never fail...
Taking law and order everywhere they go,
without fear of end they go.
And it's always great to know
they're on our side...
When the Rough Riders...
When the Rough Riders ride.

Theme Song of the Buck Jones Rangers
(sung to the tune "Over There")

Far and near, far and near
Hear the beat of our feet, far and near.
Buck Jones Rangers coming to start things humming,
We are courageous, never fear,
Unselfish, we, truthful be
As we go to our task daily.
We will stick together through all kinds of weather,
And be brave, strong Rangers,
Buck Jones Rangers, we.

The Lone Rider Theme Song

I'm the Lone Rider, on the great divide,
all alone riding, far and wide.
When a helping hand is needed,
I am ready without fail.
I'm the Lone Rider on the trail.
With a heart steady, riding on the plain,
'neath the sun or the blinding rain.
There's a job and I must do it,
and I'll do it without fail.
I'm the Lone Rider on the trail.

ROPING 'N' RIDING
WITH ALLAN "ROCKY" LANE

Howdy Pardners!

Thanks a million for the many expressions of pleasure you've sent Black Jack and me, and the friendship you've given us both. We hope we can continue to please you pards and make you happy with our comics and movies, you can bet on that.

You know, I was just thinking today of some of the great inventions that have come into being the past few years, and bothered to look up the character of some of the inventors, and you know something? Without exception they all turned out to be short on talk but mighty long-on-action kind of people, which brings me to a point.

Have you ever stopped to wonder how it is some folks can talk a blue streak and still say nothing, while other folks can pack a heap of savvy into just a few words? Those talky, talky ones seem to never get much done, do they? Nothing that counts anyway. While the other kind—the short-on-the-talk-kind—remind you of the old-timers who built up the frontiers of the west. They were mostly short on talk but mighty long on action, which is what gets things done. They didn't fritter away their time in loose talk any more than they wasted ammunition.

I call loose talk "Maverick Talk" because it sure has created a heap of trouble from time to time. You see, pards, Maverick talk can't stand up against good old savvy in a showdown, no siree.

You and I know from history that people did much loose talking about such fellows as Robert Fulton. But did that stop him? You bet it didn't. He went right ahead and built the steamboat anyway, because he was a man of action, not just a pile of words. So, if you pards have a good idea, don't let Maverick talk stop you. Go right ahead and put it into action. That's what counts today, just as it did in the early times. A little savvy will squelch a heap of nothing any old time.

Well, Pardners, Black Jack and I got to be moseying down the trail, so, so long. Take care of yourselves and we'll get together again next issue.

Yours for more action,
Your Pals,

(signed) Allan "Rocky" Lane
and his horse, Blackjack

MY MOVIE HORSE "THUNDER"
by Bill Elliott

I'd like to tell you about Thunder, and I don't mean the thunder that rumbles in the sky, but the black horse I have ridden in all the "Red Ryder" Westerns. It was quite a job to find a horse to play the role of Thunder because a horse is very important in a motion picture. A cowboy thinks a lot of his horse, and asks a lot of him. The horse must have a nice quiet disposition, must be able to run at a tremendous speed and when you bring him into a close-up, he must remain quiet so that he will not interfere with dialogue. After looking at forty or fifty black horses, I finally selected this one which I now own and call Thunder.

At every rodeo performance I will be in the arena riding Thunder and will show him in a series of his tricks. He dances, goes to the mailbox, and gets the mail for me, pushes a baby buggy, picks my hat off the ground and hands it up to me, sits down, and I put on his glasses while he holds the funny paper in his mouth and reads it. He also says his prayers and I think that it is very important that boys and girls say their prayers, and that goes for us grown-ups, too.

Thunder is a very beautiful horse in my opinion. He stands 15½ hands and weighs 1,150 pounds. I bought him from Levi Garret, of Sterling City, Texas. Thunder has traveled with me all over the United States.

In my spare time between pictures, I often take Thunder to the Children's Hospitals and entertain the boys and girls who can't get out and run and play and ride like well children can. When I take Thunder into the hospital wards, I don't even have a halter on him. He walks in and around all the kiddies and he is just as careful as can be. Lots of times I let the boys and girls ride him. I have had as many as six children on his back at once.

I think Thunder is just about the finest horse any cowboy could ever hope to own. I am very careful in what I feed him. I never give him sugar because I don't think it is good for him. He prefers carrots. They keep his hair nice and shiny and make his diet balanced. He gets a combination of hay every day, with a flake of alfalfa for breakfast and a flake of oat hay for his dinner. I have a special mixture of grain that I give him at every meal.

I have a special horse trailer in which I carry both Thunder and Stormy Night, my Quarter Horse Stallion, which I also will ride in every rodeo performance. Stormy and Thunder are always kept stabled next to each other as they are very good friends and any time I have ever seperated them, I am sure they missed one another.

There's lots more things I'd like to tell you about Thunder and Stormy, but I'd rather you'd see them yourself. I always like to talk about these two horses, so I hope the opportunity comes up soon for me to tell you some more.

WHAT AMERICA MEANS TO ME
by John Wayne

What does America mean to me? America and its people are God-fearing, hard working, honest. To me, America means Thomas Jefferson, and the Constitution, George Washington and the winter at Valley Forge, Thomas Paine and freedom, Abraham Lincoln and the freeing of the slaves, giving men human dignity no matter what the color of their skins.

It means Sam Houston, Davy Crockett, and all the men at the Alamo, and all the brave Americans who died for our country—from the American Revolution to Vietnam.

America means Iowa where I was born, Glendale, California where I grew up—old-fashioned patriotism, love of country, God, and everything decent in life.

I've been described as a flag waver, a super patriot. I plead guilty. I am all that and I don't care who knows it.

I've been all over America and I thank God every day for this country and its people, the pioneers who founded it and left the old world because they had too much character to knuckle under over there. They came over here and built a nation out of the wilderness. That takes guts, and guts is what the Americans have more than anything else.

Our revolution was not made up of dissidents and irresponsible cowards. It was made up of people who had close ties with a Mother Country. Responsible citizens who pledged their lives, their fortunes, and their sacred honor (a word that we do not seem to make important these days). They pledged all this for principle. They could have well survived under the government from which they were dissolving themselves. These were not whining dissidents. They were men of guts and honor.

To me, America means the billions of dollars that we've given to put the rest of the world on its feet. It is America who gives a damn about the world even though most of the time we get only abuse in return. Maybe there's a reason for that, too. We never were very smart about how we doled out that money.

America is our flag and what it stands for. It's a kid in the first grade with his hand over his heart reciting the pledge of allegiance.

This is my country and your country and we ought to be damn proud of it. I know I am!

COWBOY CHALLENGE

(Now that you have read this book, see how you do on the following quiz.)

1. Bob Allen and Charles Starrett graduated from what college?
2. What member of TV's GUNSMOKE was Rex Allen's cousin?
3. What is Gene Autry's biggest selling record?
4. What cowboy was turned down for the role when Bob Baker signed with Universal?
5. What was the name of Baker's horse?
6. What famous baseball star had a large role in a Smith Ballew Western?
7. Who played Little Beaver in Jim Bannon's Red Ryder films?
8. Who said, "I'm going to stay in this business until I win an Oscar"?
9. Who starred in the serial, KING OF THE TEXAS RANGERS?
10. Who played in non-westerns with Mary Pickford, JoanCrawford and Mae West?
11. Who made three different TV detective series?
12. What was the name of Rex Allen's horse?
13. Who received his screen name from a used car lot?
14. Who claimed to have sold Trigger to Roy Rogers?
15. Who took his place when Buster Crabbe left PRC?
16. Who co-wrote "Banks Of The Sunny San Juan" with Eddie Dean?
17. What cowboy's real name was Michael Harrison?
18. Who said, "I get all the westerns that Duke Wayne doesn't want"?
19. Who did John Ford scold over offering suggestions on the film FORT APACHE?
20. Who was once a pitchman for a chinchilla sales company?
21. Who got a part in GIANT because of the way he put on his hat?
22. Who claimed the contract for the Hopalong Cassidy movies was written on a piece of toilet paper?
23. Who claimed his favorite role was in THE MAGNIFICENT AMBERSONS?
24. Who was the only black B-western star?
25. Who expressed his dislike for the singing cowboys?

26. Who said about Ray Corrigan: "Actually, I didn't like the man"?
27. Who was the voice of TV's MR. ED?
28. Who had a confrontation with Hugh O'Brian on the set of WYATT EARP?
29. What member of The Three Mesquiteers had to be replaced after being injured while filming TRIGGER TRIO?
30. Who was sent to makeup to have hair removed from his hands and his eyebrows plucked?
31. Who said after several marriages: "Any sentiment about anniversaries is as cold as last year's ashes" ?
32. Who said, "I've made the same western 40 times, only with different horses"?
33. What member of The Rough Riders refused a war deferment?
34. Who claimed his family didn't care for his singing?
35. Who refused to play the part of a smart-alecky Pulitzer Prize winner who drank and smoked?
36. Who offered Reb Russell $10,000 for his horse, Rebel?
37. Who wanted to call his horse Yucca?
38. Who absolutely hated his real name?
39. Who was defeated in his bid to become senator from Tennessee?
40. Who turned down the chance to run for governor of Texas?
41. Who said, "I've never even seen a marijuana cigarette"?
42. What was the name of Charles Starrett's horse?
43. What series replaced the Cisco Kid series?
44. Al St. John got the name "Fuzzy" in what cowboy star's pictures?
45. What cowboy offered to let the studio give his raises to his sidekick?
46. What was the name of Lash LaRue's horse?
47. Who told the studio that the Lone Ranger role was stupid?
48. Who got his famous nickname from a dog?
49. Who was accused of copying Gene Autry?
50. Black Jack O'Shea toured the country with what cowboy star?
51. Whose football team accepted the Rose Bowl bid after Charles Starrett's team turned it down?
52. What was the name of Fred Scott's horse?
53. What was the name of Tex Ritter's horse?

54. Who was asked to grow a beard after being seen working with a fake one?
55. Who said, "Horses are dangerous at both ends"?
56. What sidekick was let go by George O'Brien?
57. Who said he probably got his nickname because he was round and short?
58. Who told Slim Andrews that he would not be in any more of Gene Autry's films?
59. Who said. "By the grace of God and Gene Autry I got a career"?
60. Whose horse ran away with him while being checked out by the studio?
61. Dorothy Fay was married to what cowboy hero?
62. Who came out of retirement to make the serial, THE MIRACLE RIDER?
63. What cowboy star's daughter asked her step-mother to quit smoking?
64. Cecila Parker asked what cowboy to behave himself and curb his language?
65. Who did Hank Bell say was the best rider in the business?
66. What cowboy did Marshall Reed say was like a "rock"?
67. Who once dated Rita Hayworth?
68. Who was the assistant cameraman when Buck Jones made his first film for Fox?
69. Whose mother cried when she saw the film, SONG OF OLD WYOMING?
70. Who bought 2000 acres and turned it into a movie location?
71. What was the name of Sunset Carson's horse?
72. Who credited John Wayne and Mickey Rooney with getting him into movies?
73. Who bought Bob Baker's horse when Baker left Hollywood?
74. What badman lost part of his hand while working with dynamite?
75. Who was taught to handle a gun by former bank robber Al Jennings?
76. Who was a Presbyterian minister before entering films?
77. Who did Peggy Stewart call "Bubble-Butt"?
78. Whose real name was George Duryea?
79. Who divorced his wife and married his mother-in-law?
80. Who was originally scheduled to star in DON'T FENCE ME IN?

ANSWERS TO COWBOY CHALLENGE

1. Dartmouth
2. Glenn Strange
3. Rudolph the Red-Nosed Reindeer
4. Roy Rogers
5. Apache
6. Lou Gehrig
7. Don Kay Reynolds
8. Don Barry
9. Sammy Baugh
10. Johnny Mack Brown
11. Rod Cameron
12. Koko
13. Sunset Carson
14. Ray Corrigan
15. Lash LaRue
16. Glenn Strange
17. Sunset Carson
18. Bill Elliott
19. Dick Foran
20. Hoot Gibson
21. Monte Hale
22. Russell Hayden
23. Tim Holt
24. Herb Jeffries
25. Buck Jones
26. John "Dusty" King
27. Allan "Rocky" Lane
28. Lash LaRue
29. Bob Livingston
30. Ken Maynard
31. Tom Mix
32. Audie Murphy
33. Tim McCoy
34. Tex Ritter
35. Roy Rogers
36. Bob Wills
37. Charles Starrett
38. John Wayne
39. Tex Ritter
40. Eddie Dean
41. Roy Rogers
42. Raider
43. Jimmy Wakely
44. Fred Scott
45. Tim Holt
46. Black Diamond
47. Jim Bannon
48. John Wayne
49. Jimmy Wakely
50. Bob Steele
51. Johnny Mack Brown
52. White Dust
53. White Flash
54. Gabby Hayes
55. Pat Buttram
56. Chill Wills
57. Cannonball Taylor
58. Smiley Burnette
59. Jimmy Wakely
60. Whip Wilson
61. Tex Ritter
62. Tom Mix
63. Roy Rogers
64. Ken Maynard
65. Ken Maynard
66. Rocky Lane
67. Tex Ritter
68. George O'Brien
69. Lash LaRue
70. Ray Corrigan
71. Cactus
72. Don Barry
73. Montie Montana
74. Fred Kohler Sr.
75. Tex Ritter
76. Fred Thomson
77. Rocky Lane
78. Tom Keene
79. Rod Cameron
80. Monte Hale

———————————————

How do you rate?

75-80 .... hero in white hat
70-74 .... faithful sidekick
below 70 .... dirty desperado
who needs to read
this book again!

Index

ABOUT THE AUTHOR

Among B-western aficionados there are the passive and the active. To keep the interest in Saturday matinee western heroes alive we desperately need both. The passive to read, watch and collect. The active to write, research, locate and preserve long lost films, stage film festivals and publish books and periodicals on westerns. Bobby Copeland is among the most active. That fact is proven once again with publication of this, his first, book. Hundreds of hours of diligent research went into seeking out these many interesting celebrity quotes.

Over the years Bobby has had dozens of articles on B-westerns published in WRANGLER'S ROOST, UNDER WESTERN SKIES, CLASSIC IMAGES, THE WESTERNER, CLIFFHANGER, FAVORITE WESTERNS, SAGEBRUSH JOURNAL and others. For over a year he has been a regular columnist for our WESTERN CLIPPINGS. He was a co-founder of the Knoxville, TN, "Riders of the Silver Screen," serving five times as their president. He continues to write and edit their interesting newsletter. In 1988 Bobby received the "Buck Jones Rangers Trophy," presented annually to individuals demonstrating consistent dedication to keeping the spirit of the B-western alive. In 1994 Don Key (Empire Publishing) and I awarded Bobby the "Buck Rainey Shoot 'Em Ups Pioneer Award" which yearly honors a fan who has contributed beyond the norm to the hobby of film collecting preservation.

Within the pages of TRAIL TALK Bobby has sought carefully to present factual quotes from every possible B-western notable. Issued over the years at film festivals, in books or through personal interviews, these quotes serve to present a well-rounded portrait of what our screen heroes were like and how they viewed one another. Reading the quotes in TRAIL TALK you come away realizing the love and respect these stars had for the movies they made. Obviously that's why we revere and respect them as we do. We thank Bobby for bringing them all together in one volume.

Boyd Magers
Video West, Inc/WESTERN CLIPPINGS

Other Movie / TV Books Available from Empire Publishing:

1001 Toughest TV Trivia Questions of All Time by Vincent Terrace
Allan "Rocky" Lane, Republic's Action Ace by Chuck Thornton and David Rothel
The Allied Artists Checklist by Len D. Martin
America on the Rerun by David Story
An Ambush of Ghosts by David Rothel
Award Winning Films by Peter C. Mowrey
Best of Universal by Tony Thomas
Betty Grable: The Girl with the Million Dollar Legs by Tom McGee
The Beverly Hillbillies
Black Hollywood by Gary Null
Black Hollywood: From 1960 to Today by Gary Null
The Brady Bunch Book by Andrew J. Eledstein and Frank Lovece
Bugsy by James Toback
B-Western Actors Encyclopedia by Ted Holland
Candid Cowboys, Vols. 1 & 2 by Neil Summers
Cartoon Movie Posters by Bruce Hershenson
Charlie Chan and the Movies by Ken Hanke
The "Cheers" Trivia Book by Mark Wenger
Child Star by Chirley Temple Black
Classic TV Westerns by Ronald Jackson
Classics of the Gangster Film by Robert Bookbinder
Classics of the Horror Film by Williams K. Everson
C'mon Get Happy by David Cassidy
The Columbia Checklist by Len D. Martin
Complete Films of Audrey Hepburn
Complete Films of Bela Lugosi by Richard Bojarski
Complete Films of Bette Davis by Gene Ringgold
Complete Films of Cary Grant by Donald Deschner
Complete Films of Cecil B. DeMille by Gene Ringgold and DeWitt Bodeen
Complete Films of Charlie Chaplin by Gerald D. McDonald
Complete Films of Clark Gable by Gabe Essoe
Complete Films of Edward G. Robinson by Alvin H. Marill
Complete Films of Erroll Flynn by Tony Thomas, et al
Complete Films of Frank Capra by Victor Scherle & William Turner Levy
Complete Films of Gary Cooper by Homer Dickens
Complete Films of Henry Fonda by Tony Thomas
Complete Films of Ingrid Bergman by Lawrence J. Quirk
Complete Films of James Cagney by Homer C. Dickens
Complete Films of Jeanette MacDonald and Nelson Eddy by Philip Castanza
Complete Films of Joan Crawford by Lawrence J. Quirk
Complete Films of John Huston by John McCarty
Complete Films of John Wayne by Mark Ricci, et al
Complete Films of Judy Garland by Joe Morella and Edward Z Epstein
Complete Films of Laurel & Hardy by William K. Everson
Complete Films of Mae West by Jon Tuska
Complete Films of Marilyn Monroe by Michael Conway and Mark Ricci
Complete Films of Marlene Dietrich by Homer Dickens
Complete Films of the Marx Brothers by Allen Eyles
Complete Films of Orson Wells by James Howard
Complete Films of Rita Hayworth by Gene Ringgold
Complete Films of Spencer Tracy by Donald Deschner
Complete Films of Steve McQueen by Casey St. Chamez
Complete Films of W. C. Fields by Donald Deschner
Complete Films of William Holden by Lawrence J. Quirk
Complete Films of William Powell by Lawrence J. Quirk
Cowboy Movie Posters by Bruce Hershenson
The Cowboy and the Kid by J. Brim Crow III and Jack H. Smith
Cult Horror Films by Everman

Curly by Joan Howard Maurer
The Cutting Room Floor by Laurent Bouzereau
A Darling of the Twenties: Madge Bellamy
Dave's WorldThe Dick Powell Story by Tony Thomas
Dick Tracy: America's Most Famous Detective edited by Bill Crouch, Jr.
The Disney Films by Leonard Maltin
Divine Images by Roy Kinnard and Tim Davis
Don Miller's Hollwood Corral by Smith & Hulse
Early Classics of the Foreign Film by Parker Tyler
Elvis: A Celebration in Pictures by Charles Hirshbergh and the editors of *Life*
Evenings with Cary Grant by Nance Nelson
Famous Hollywood Locations by Leon Smith
Fantastic Cinema Subject Guide
Favorite Families of TV
Feature Players: The Stories Behind the Faces, Vol. 2 by Jim & Tom Goldrup
The FIlm Encyclopedia
Film Flubs by Bill Givens
Films and Career of Elvis by Steven Zmijewsky and Boris Zmijewski
Films Flubs, The Sequal by Bill Givens
Films of Alfred Hitchcock by Robert A. Harris and Michael S. Lasky
Films of Al Pacino by Schoell
Films of Arnold Schwarzenegger by John L. Flynn
Films of Carole Lombard by Fred W. Ott
Films of Clint Eastwood by Boris Zmijewsky and Lee Pfeiffer
Films of Dustin Hoffman by Douglas Brode
Films of Elizabeth Taylor by Jerry Vermilye and Aldo Vigano
Films of Federico Fellini by Claudio Fava & Aldo Vigano
Films of Frank Sinatra by Gene Ringgold and Clifford McCarty
Films of Gina Lollobrigida by Maurizio Ponzi
Films of Gloria Swanson by Lawrence J. Quirk
Films of Gregory Peck by John Griggs
Films of Greta Garbo by Conway et al
Films of Hopalong Cassidy by Francis M. Nevins, Jr.
Films of Jack Nicholson by Douglas Brode
Films of Jane Fonda by George Hadley-Garcia
Films of Katharine Hepburn by Homer Dickens
Films of Kirk Douglas by Tony Thomas
Films of Lauren Bacall by Lawrence J. Quirk
Films of Laurence Olivier by Margaret Morley
Films of Marlon Brando by Tony Thomas
Films of Merchant Ivory by Long
Films of Norma Shearer by Jack Jacobs and Myron Braum
Films of Olivia DeHavilland by Tony Thomas
Films of Paul Newman by Lawrence J. Quirk
Films of Peter Lorre by Stephen D. Youngkin, James Bigwood, and Raymond Cabana, Jr.
Films of Robert DeNiro by Douglas Brode
Films of Robert Redford by James Spada
Films of Sean Connery by Lee Pfeiffer and Phillip Lisa
Films of Shirley MacLaine by Christopher Paul Denis
Films of Shirley Temple by Robert Windeler
Films of Steven Spielberg by Douglas Brode
Films of the Eighties by Douglas Brode
Films of the Fifties by Douglas Brode
Films of the Seventies by Robert Bookbinder
Films of the Sixties by Douglas Brode
Films of the Thirties by Jerry Vermilye
Films of Warren Beatty by Lawrence Quirk
Films of Woody Allen by Douglas Brode
Final Curtain: Deaths of Noted Movie & TV Personalities
First Films by Jami Bernard

Northern Exposure Book: The Official Publication of the Television of the Television Series by Louis Chunovic
Northern Exposures by Rob Morrow
Official Andy Griffith Show Scrapbook by Lee Pfeiffer
The Official Dick Van Dyke Show by Vince Waldron
Official John Wayne Reference Book by Charles John Kieskalt
Official TV Western Book, Vols. 1, 2,3, & 4 by Neil Summers
Old Familiar Faces by Robert A. Juran
Partridge Family Album by Joey Green
Poverty Row Horrors by Tom Weaver
Randolph Scott / A Film Biography by Jefferson Brim Crow, III
The Real Bob Steele and a Man Called Brad by Bob Nareau
The Republic Chapterplays by R. M. Hayes
Republic Confidential: Volume2 - The Players by Jack Mathis
Riding the Video Range by Gary A. Yoggy
The RKO Features by James L. Neibaur
The Round-Up by Donald R. Key
Round Up the Usual Suspects by Aljean Harmetz
Roy Rogers by Robert W. Philllips
Roy Rogers Reference-Trivia-Scrapbook by David Rothel
Saddle Gals by Edgar M. Wyatt and Steve Turner
Saddle Pals by Garv Towell and Wayne E. Keates
Saddle Serenaders by Guy Logsdon, Mary Rogers and William Jacobson
Second Feature by John Cocchi
Serials-ly Speaking by William C. Cline
The Shoot-em-Ups Ride Again by Buck Rainey
Silent Film Necrology by Eugene Michael Vazzana
Silent Portraits by Anthony Slide
Sinatra Scrapbook by Gary L. Doctor
Singing Cowboy Stars by Robert Phillips
Son of Film Flubs by Bill Givens
Speaking of Silents: First Ladies of the Screen by William Drew
Star Trek Movie Memories by William Shatner
Stroke of Fortune by William C. Cline
Sunday Nights at Seven: The Jack Benny Story by Jack Benny and daughter Joan
Television Westerns by Richard West
They Sang! They Danced! They Romanced! by John Springer
They Still Call Me Junior by Frank "Junior" Coghlan
Those Fabulous Serial Heroines by Buck Rainey
Three Stooges Scrapbook by Jeff Lenburg, Joan Howard Maurer, Greg Lenburg
Thrillers: Seven Decades of Classic Film Suspense by John McCarthy
Tim Holt by David Rothel
Tom Mix: a Heavily-Illustrated Biography by Paul E. Mix
Tom Mix Book by M. G. "Bud" Norris
Tom Mix Highlights by Andy Woytowch
Tom Mix: The Formative Years by Paul E. Mix
Universal Horrors by Tom Weaver
Ultimate John Wayne Trivia Book
Ultimate Unauthorized Star Trek Quiz Book by Robert W. Bly
Valley of the Cliffhangers Supplement by Jack Mathis
The Vanishing Legion by John Tucka*West That Never Was* by Tony Thomas
Wayne's World: Extreme Close-up by Mike Myers and Robin Ruzan
Way Out West by Jane and Michael Stern
Western Films of John Ford by J. A. Place
Whatever Happened to Randolph Scott? by C. H. Scott
Who Is That? by Warren B. Meyers
Wizard of Oz: The Official 50th Anniversary Pictorial History by John Fricke, Jay Scarfone, and William Stillman
Words and Shadows by Jim Hitt
You Ain't Heard Nothin' Yet by John P. Fennell